OXFORD

Framework
non-FICTION

Richard Broomhead

Great Clarendon Street, Oxford OX2 6DP

Oxford University Press is a department of the University of Oxford.
It furthers the University's objective of excellence in research, scholarship,
and education by publishing worldwide in

Oxford New York

Athens Auckland Bangkok Bogotá Buenos Aires Kolkata
Cape Town Chennai Dar es Salaam Delhi Florence Hong Kong Istanbul
Karachi Kuala Lumpur Madrid Melbourne Mexico City Mumbai
Nairobi Paris São Paulo Shanghai Singapore Taipei Tokyo Toronto Warsaw

with associated companies in Berlin Ibadan

Oxford is a registered trade mark of Oxford University Press
in the UK and in certain other countries

ISBN 0 19 831467 1

Printed in Spain

Contents

Everything we write is for someone to read – that is, it has an audience. We also always have a purpose (the reason we are writing it: to inform our audience, or entertain them, for example). We match our writing to our audience and purpose – we have to think about both these things to get it right.

Writing for a purpose

This list shows you some of the purposes of speaking and writing:

inform	explain	describe	report
argue	persuade	instruct	review
analyse	comment	advise	summarize
entertain	narrate	imagine	explore

Some texts have several purposes, for example:

A tabloid newspaper report might aim to:

- report (tell facts)
- summarize
- recount (tell a story)
- entertain (as its style is informal, chatty and almost like gossip).

Or an advert's purpose might be to:

- argue – 'because you're worth it'
- persuade – 'it's the best choice'
- instruct – 'buy today!'

Look at these examples and decide, using the list above, on the purpose for each one (remember, some might have more than one purpose).

1

The snowman was amazed by everything he saw. They even went into James' mother and father's bedroom. And the snowman dressed up in their clothes. Suddenly, the snowman took James by the hand and ran out of the house, across the snow, and up, up into the air. They were flying!

2

GLADIATOR

– this will, without doubt, be the great cinematic roller-coaster ride of the year, a spectacular event to rival, if you like, Titanic – but with this difference: Gladiator makes Titanic look about as thrilling as if the ship had sunk in dry dock with nobody on board.

3

For those used to the HIGH life, the PISCIS PARK is as high as a kite. The hotel is quite simply fantastic – providing everything the 2wentys massive needs from their accommodation. After wearing out your trainers all night, this place will soothe you back to reality, with its wicked pool and bar area. This place has the BEST position in resort – Es Paradis and Eden could not be closer and the views over the bay are just wicked.

4

STRAW'S JAG IS NICKED AT 103 mph

Jack Straw was stopped by cops who caught his Jaguar doing 103mph on the M5.

5

Are your children safe in the kitchen? Every day 10 small children under the age of 5 are severely burnt or scalded in the home.

- Keep the handles of pots and pans turned away from the edges of cookers and work surfaces
- Teach toddlers not to play in the kitchen or bathroom. Check for toys you might trip over.

6

Volcanoes happen where magma from inside the Earth forces its way up through cracks or holes in the Earth's crust. Magma that comes out of a volcano is called lava. It cools and hardens, making new igneous rocks.

7

First break two eggs and whisk together.
Next, add 200g of flour and fold slowly.
Then add in the orange flavouring.
Finally, add sugar and milk and mix in well.

8

Why should a fox be chased for hours on end, only to be brutally killed by a pack of marauding dogs and watched by narrow-minded imbeciles on horseback? Fox hunting is a barbaric sport and has no place in a modern and so-called civilized society.

Now compare your ideas as a class.

- What made it easy to say what the purpose was for some of the examples?

- Why were some more difficult to place?

Writing for an audience

The audience – who a text is for – is another important factor in writing a text. Here are examples 1 and 3 again. What clues tell you who their audience is?

Example 1

> The snowman was amazed by everything he saw. They even went into James' mother and father's bedroom. And the snowman dressed up in their clothes. Suddenly, the snowman took James by the hand and ran out of the house, across the snow, and up, up into the air. They were flying!

a Are the sentences long or short? Are they straightforward or complicated?

b How much detail does the writer provide about the scene?

c Are the words easy or difficult to understand?

Example 3

> **For those used to the HIGH life, the PISCIS PARK is as high as a kite. The hotel is quite simply fantastic – providing everything the 2wentys massive needs from their accommodation. After wearing out your trainers all night, 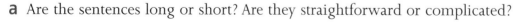 this place will soothe you back to reality, with its wicked pool and bar area. This place has the BEST position in resort – Es Paradis and Eden could not be closer and the views over the bay are just wicked.**

a Are the sentences long or short? Are they straightforward or complicated?

b Is the language formal or chatty? (Look at words like 'wicked'.)

c What is the pace of the writing like? Does it sound fast and exciting or slow and leisurely?

One way of deciding on the audience is to look at the types of sentences the writer uses. You need to use appropriate sentence types to suit your audience. For instance, if example 1 were written in a more complex way, a young child could not follow it.

There are three main types of sentences:

Simple

A simple sentence contains one main idea, for example:

They even went into James' mother and father's bedroom.

They were flying!

Compound

A compound sentence contains two or more ideas joined by the conjunctions 'and', 'or' or 'but', for example:

Suddenly, the snowman took James by the hand and ran out of the house, across the snow, and up, up into the air.

Complex

A complex sentence contains more than one idea and can be made up of several clauses. One clause is the main clause, which deals with the main meaning of the sentence. There will also be one or more subordinate clauses, which give more information about what is happening, for example:

Although it was a cold morning, the sun was shining brightly in the sky.

subordinate clause
(adds another action to the sentence but would not make sense on its own)

main clause
(makes sense on its own)

Look at these examples of different types of sentence:

1 Spot barked. He was happy. He liked going for walks.

2 The police raced along the motorway but could not catch up with the stolen car and soon lost track of its whereabouts.

3 Even though he had been there before, he was unsure if it resembled its former glory, and too many painful memories darted through his mind, making him want to leave at once.

What can you tell about a possible audience for each text, based on the type of sentence used?

Register

Register is about how formally you express yourself: it is a combination of the kinds of sentences and words you use. Slang belongs to a very informal register, for example.

What register you use depends on your audience and the situation. For example, you would use an informal register with your friends, but if you were talking to the Queen you would probably use a much more formal register.

Look at this example of speech:

> Would you mind closing the window?

This seems rather formal and polite. The speaker asks 'would you mind' and uses a formal verb 'closing'. Look at these variations on the same idea:

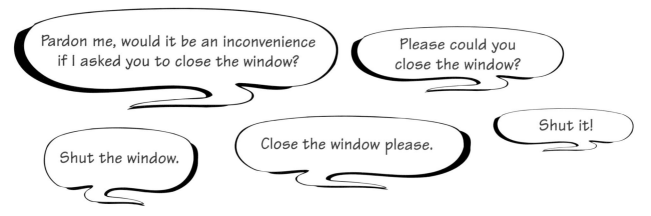

> Pardon me, would it be an inconvenience if I asked you to close the window?

> Please could you close the window?

> Shut it!

> Close the window please.

> Shut the window.

In a small group, rank these in order of formality – with the most formal at the top and the least formal at the bottom.

Now decide who would be a suitable audience for each statement. (For example, would you say the first one to a brother or sister?)

Compare your ideas now as a whole class.

Now look at this letter where the writer is using the wrong register – his tone, style and sentence types are all wrong. It really shows he has not got much sense of his audience.

Rotherham, South Yorkshire

Dear Mister,

I want to work with your company because I am good at selling things and making money (and that is what you are in business for right?) I have just left school and think that I might do quite well in my GCSE's but I could have done a bit more revision. When can I come in for an interview about my job? Can't wait to hear from you.

Cheers
Karl Martin

Imagine you receive this letter as the manager of the company. Why would you NOT want to meet Karl? What advice could you give him to improve his letter? Make suggestions for how he could improve the:

a layout of the letter

b use of sentence types

c sense of audience

d vocabulary

e tone.

As you can see from Karl's letter, using inappropriate language for your audience can be disastrous.

So, unlike Karl, we usually adapt our language and style depending on three things:

- what our purpose is
- who our audience is and how well we know them – we need to consider what we say (content), and how we say it (our use of language, vocabulary, grammar, register and tone)
- what the topic is.

Remember to think about these things whenever you write a text – and when you are reading one. It can tell you a lot about why the writer is using language in the way they are.

Step by step

Instructions are a feature of modern life. We use them to find out how to do things, how to use equipment, and as guides to rules, like the highway code. Think about the sort of times that we use instructions:

- in talk – who do you get instructions from? where are you likely to get them?

- in reading – think about instructional texts around school walls, in food technology, etc.

 Exploring instructions

Look at the map on page 13, and find points **A** and **B** on it. Imagine you are at point **A**. Write down instructions for a friend to reach point **B**.

What do you notice about what you have written? Have you:

- used the imperative (command form) by saying things such as 'turn left and go straight on'?

- kept your instructions short and clear?

- given your instructions in the order they should be followed (chronological order)?

- used temporal markers, for example '**first** turn left, **next** go **right**, **after this** go straight on'?

If you haven't, have another look at your instructions now and see if you can improve them by doing these things.

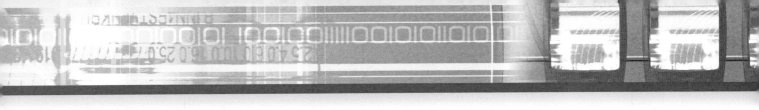

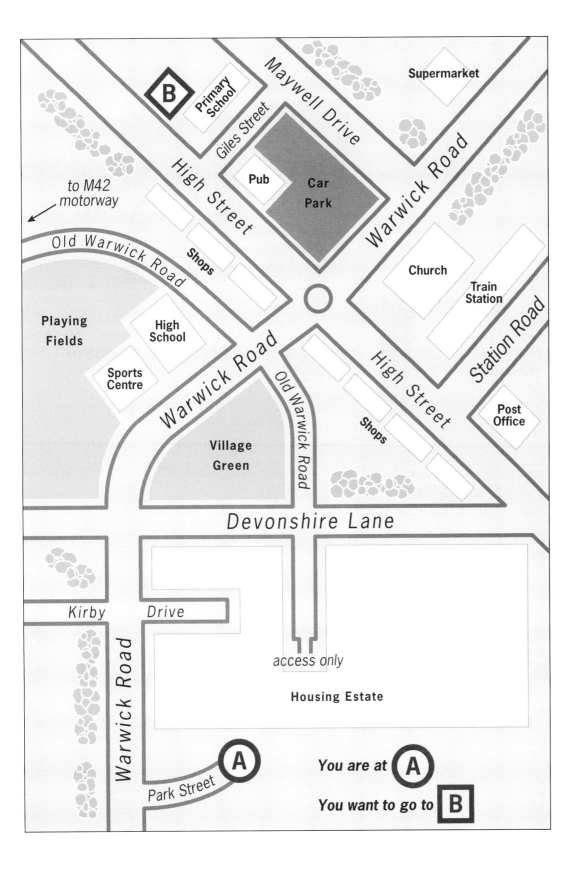

Now look at these examples of instructional texts. What do they have in common? Think about:

a the length of each instruction

b how the reader is told what to do

c what order the instructions are given in

d how the sequence of instructions is made clear.

A

999 Know what you can do if someone gets really drowsy:

- **Calm them and be reassuring.**
- **NEVER give coffee to rouse them.**
- **If symptoms persist, place them in the recovery position.**
- **Call an ambulance if necessary.**

B

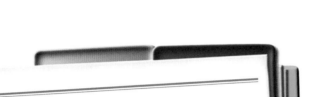

1 **Empty contents into a pan.**
2 **Mix in a quarter of a pint of milk.**
3 **Bring to the boil and stir continuously.**
4 **Simmer for 15 minutes.**

C

Before you switch the power on, read this booklet.

Then switch DVD player on ensuring that the red light glows on the display panel.

Next, press 'eject' button and place DVD disc on and insert.

Now take remote control and press the track number, then 'enter'.

🔑 The key to writing instructions

Instructional texts need to be clear and easy to follow. So when you are writing instructions, make sure that you:

- write short, clear sentences

- give the instructions in the order they need to be followed in (chronological order)

- make the sequence clear: divide the instructions with bullet points, numbers or words (discourse markers) like 'before…', 'next', 'then'

- tell the reader what to do through the imperative (command) form of the verb ('calm them', 'mix in', 'press').

Fire safety leaflet

This leaflet was devised by the British government to tell people what to do in case of a fire at home.

GET A PLAN

GET OUT ALIVE

FIRE KILLS
YOU CAN PREVENT IT

FL5 Pubished by Home Office. March 00

What to do if you have a Fire

If your smoke alarm goes off, put your plan into action without delay:

Raise the alarm

- Get everyone together and make your way out of the building by your planned escape route. Don't attempt to rescue pets or valuables.

Check doors with the back of your hand

- If a door feels warm don't open it. A closed door provides protection from fire. Do not open doors as this can allow the fire to spread.

If there's a lot of smoke

- Crawl along with your nose close to the floor, where there is usually an area of clean air.

If your escape route is blocked, or you live above the first floor level

- Get everyone into one room. Smoke and fumes can kill quickly, so make the room safe. Close the door, put bedding or towels along the bottom of the door to keep out smoke and open the window.
- Use a telephone or mobile to call the Fire Brigade, or shout for help from the window.
- Stay by the window near the fresh air. Firefighters will also be able to see you and get to you quickly.

If you have to escape from a window

- If it won't open you'll need to break it. Break double-glazing by hitting it in the bottom corner with a sharp object.
- Carefully break away jagged glass and put thick bedding over the sill for protection.
- Throw cushions, pillows or bedding down below to break your fall.
- If you have children, elderly or infirm people with you, plan the order of escape so that they can be helped down.
- Don't jump – lower yourself down until you are hanging from the window ledge before letting go.

Call the Fire Brigade on 999

- From the nearest telephone, either from a neighbour's house or a telephone kiosk. State clearly the address of the fire.

Don't go back inside

- A firefighter will tell you when it's safe to do so.

(!) **If the smoke alarm goes off don't investigate – Get out.**

Text level focus

1 This sort of text needs to look appealing and easy to read. Which of these presentational devices have been used to do this?

- picture
- colour
- bold writing
- headings
- boxes
- bullet points
- short paragraphs
- title
- border

2 Sequence: is the text all written in chronological order? Why do you think it has been done in this way?

3 Good instructional texts use simple, uncomplicated vocabulary. Does this example? Why do you think simple language has been used?

4 Bullet points, numbers and discourse markers can be used to guide the reader through the instructions in order. The writer of this text has used bullet points, but not numbers or discourse markers.

Look at this example from the leaflet:

Raise the alarm
- *Get everyone together and make your way out of the building by your planned escape route.*

This could also be written as:

Raise the alarm
First, get everyone together and then make your way out of the building by your planned escape route.

Both versions tell the reader the same thing but they are organized slightly differently. Which one do you think is clearer and why?

5 Why do you think the writer uses subheadings such as 'Raise the alarm' and 'If there's a lot of smoke'?

6 How successful do you think these instructions are? Could they be improved? Think about:

a presentational devices and layout – is it well presented and attractive?

b the use of discourse markers – is it easy to follow the sequence?

FIRE KILLS

YOU CAN PREVENT IT

Sentence level focus

1 Instructional texts are normally written in the imperative (command form of the verb).

a Which of these examples are in the imperative?

- Raise the alarm
- If there's a lot of smoke
- Get everyone into one room
- Shout for help from the window

b Copy out the imperative from the correct examples. Then find three more examples of the imperative in the text.

2 Most of the sentences in instructions are simple or compound.

a Find an example of each of these types of sentence in the text.

b Now look at this example, where two simple sentences have been changed into a complex sentence:

If a closed door is warm, do not open it as it provides protection from the fire.

Do you think complex sentences are suitable for this text type? Why?

Simple sentences contain one idea, e.g. Raise the alarm.

Compound sentences contain two or more ideas, joined by 'and', 'but', or 'or', e.g.
Phone the Fire Brigade or shout for help.

Complex sentences are made up of a main clause (which would make sense on its own) and one or more subordinate clauses (which add more information but could not stand alone) e.g.
Never panic, although you may be tempted to.

main clause   subordinate clause
(works on its own)   (more information,
                     but doesn't work on its own)

3 Instructional texts can use adverbial phrases to give more information to the reader following the steps.

Copy out the chart and write these adverbial phrases from the text in the right columns.

'How' phrases	'When' phrases	'Where' phrases

a without delay
b by your planned escape route
c with the back of your hand
d with your nose close to the floor
e above the first floor level
f into one room
g along the bottom of the door
h from the window
i by the window
j in the bottom corner
k over the sill
l until you are hanging from the window ledge

An adverbial phrase is a group of words which tells us how, when, or where something is done, e.g.
she screamed at the top of her voice – how
she stopped after a moment – when
she ran into the house – where

Word level focus

1 This type of text needs to be clear and simple. Instructions tend to explain what to do using mainly verbs and nouns, e.g.

Stay by the window.

verb   noun

Copy out the chart. Then look at these examples and sort the verbs and nouns into your copy.

Verbs	Nouns

- break double-glazing
- throw cushions
- do not open doors
- crawl along with your nose close to the floor
- use a telephone or mobile

Writing instructions

Design an instruction sheet for the general public on one of these topics:

- how to record a television programme on video using the timer
- how to send an e-mail
- how to tie a tie
- how to cook or prepare a certain food or meal.

Research and planning

- Choose a subject that you already know enough about.
- You only have one page in which to present everything – decide which are the main points needed.

Advice on structure and language

- You might want to use diagrams, labels, and captions to help the reader.
- Set it out clearly and in order – use subheadings to divide the instructions if necessary.

- Use discourse markers, numbers or bullet points to make the sequence clear.
- Use the imperative form of the verb.
- Remember that simple and compound sentences are easiest to understand.
- Use adverbial phrases if you need to give more detail.

Drafting

- Keep checking that your instructions are clear and easy to follow.
- Check that the language level is right – remember that this is aimed at all ages.

Revising

- Check the sequence and presentation.
- Make sure that your instructions are short and to the point.
- Get a friend to try them out, then change anything that doesn't work.

Good advice

Advice is something that we give and receive all the time.

How do you give good advice?

 Exploring advice

Look at this letter to a problem page and the two replies to it.

Dear Jill,

My parents won't let me grow up and I've had enough. Imagine the embarrassment of being met at school, getting driven everywhere and being banned from having mates round. I can't even use the phone. I'm sick of it all. Help.

Robbie Williams fan, 14

Reply 1

Dear Robbie Williams fan,

Stop your moaning. Just invite your mates round – your mum and dad are hardly going to cause a scene in front of them. Buy a mobile phone – that'll solve your problems if you want to call your mates up. Failing all else, run away from home and rough it on the streets – that'll teach them a lesson!

Jill

Reply 2

Dear Robbie Williams fan,

Parents often find it hard to accept that their children grow up. There will be a cross-over period when they might occasionally treat you like a child, but this will pass. Try talking to them in a calm and reasonable way about how you feel. Explain how embarrassed you sometimes feel, and see if you can reach an agreement together about what you can and can't do. Perhaps having friends round once a week to begin with might be a way of building your parents' trust in you. Try to agree on what is acceptable in terms of using the telephone and what they think is too much. And put your point of view across. If you don't make some attempt to talk and explain, then things will never improve. Remember, your parents are probably doing their best. Good luck.

Jill

Look at Jill's two replies again and think about their style.
Answer these questions for each one.

a Is it sympathetic or unsympathetic?

b Is its advice practical or impractical?

c Is it written in a friendly way?

Now decide: which one is the best piece of advice?

So the best advice is sympathetic, practical and written in a friendly style.
Read these next two advice texts. Which one is friendliest in its tone?

A

Advice on sunbathing

Do not stay out for hours on end – you'll get
sunstroke and be ill for days.
Do not look directly into the sun because
it will blind you.
Forget to put on sun-cream and you'll be
burned to a frazzle.

B

Starting a new school

Starting a new school can be pretty
stressful but it needn't be. Everyone
at your new school understands
how worried you will be, after all
they were new once too. Being
prepared for the first day is one step towards being more relaxed
about it. Check that you know
what time school starts, see who's
also going from your previous
school, talk to other people who
are already at the school.

Think about these two texts in more detail.
Answer these questions for each one:

a Is it positive or negative in its advice?

b Does it try to reassure the reader?

c Is it more like a series of instructions than advice?

 # The key to writing advice

So how do you write good advice? Always try to make it friendly by:

- giving helpful, practical suggestions
- being positive, not negative
- trying to reassure your reader.

Good advice blends instructions with discussion so that the reader
or listener feels at ease and able to act on what is said.

Tackling Stress Mentally

This advice is from a psychologist's website offering advice to students on exam stress.

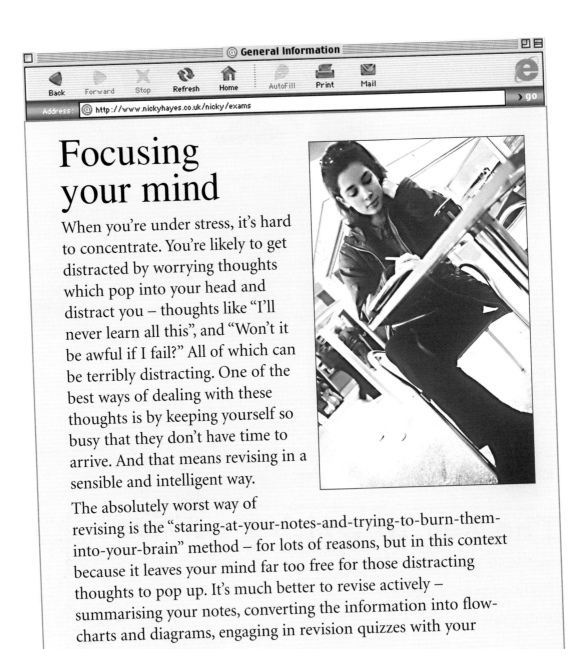

@ General Information

Back Forward Stop Refresh Home AutoFill Print Mail

Address: @ http://www.nickyhayes.co.uk/nicky/exams › go

Focusing your mind

When you're under stress, it's hard to concentrate. You're likely to get distracted by worrying thoughts which pop into your head and distract you – thoughts like "I'll never learn all this", and "Won't it be awful if I fail?" All of which can be terribly distracting. One of the best ways of dealing with these thoughts is by keeping yourself so busy that they don't have time to arrive. And that means revising in a sensible and intelligent way.

The absolutely worst way of revising is the "staring-at-your-notes-and-trying-to-burn-them-into-your-brain" method – for lots of reasons, but in this context because it leaves your mind far too free for those distracting thoughts to pop up. It's much better to revise actively – summarising your notes, converting the information into flow-charts and diagrams, engaging in revision quizzes with your

@ General Information

Back   Forward   Stop   Refresh   Home   AutoFill   Print   Mail   go

Address   @ http://www.nickyhayes.co.uk/nicky/exams

friends, and so on. By doing that, your mind will be too busy for these thoughts to come up. There are good mental reasons for doing this too – it helps you to learn better – but they're for the Revision Page.

If you have ever tried yoga or meditation, you'll know that it's possible to confine your awareness to a much more narrow focus than you normally use. Use the same exercises to screen out awareness of everything but the problem that you are working on. Although it can sometimes be tiring, really deep concentration, with all of the distractions screened out, can also be tremendously refreshing.

To achieve that, though, you actually need to be interested in your work. It's hard to concentrate fully on something that you find boring. But nothing really needs to be boring – not if you explore all of its implications. Try discussing the topic with other people – friends, parents, teachers – to find out why it matters. If you listen to what they say with an open mind, you'll probably get some unusual insights, which will help you to focus on your revision with more interest. Of course, it does need an open mind – if you've already decided that the topic is simply dull, then nobody will be able to change your mind for you.

Good advice

Text level focus

1 This sort of text should use paragraphs to make the advice flow in a logical way. Look at how paragraph 1 ends – it talks about 'revising in a sensible and intelligent way'.

Paragraph 2 begins 'the absolutely worst way of revising is…'

So the idea of revising well makes a link between the paragraphs. See if you can find this sort of link between other paragraphs.

2 How can you tell that this advice is aimed at students?

3 Which words would you use to describe the style of this text?

- informative
- chatty
- reassuring
- friendly
- patronizing
- personal

Can you back up your choices with examples from the text?

Sentence level focus

1 Many of the sentences in this text are complex sentences, like:

When you're under stress, it's hard to concentrate.

a Find another example of a complex sentence.

Complex sentences are made up of a main clause (which would make sense on its own) and one or more subordinate clauses (which add more information but could not stand alone) e.g.

I visited my aunt and cousins, who live in New York.

main clause (works on its own)

subordinate clause (more information, but doesn't work on its own)

Sometimes complex sentences can have more than one subordinate clause, e.g.

Although grandma is old, she's funny, so she is good company.

subordinate clause   main clause   subordinate clause

b Why do you think the writer uses complex sentences in this text?

- to make the advice sound clever
- to confuse the reader
- because the advice is aimed at more advanced readers
- because the writer doesn't like simple sentences

2 The writer gives some advice in the imperative – the command form of the verb: 'get up', 'please listen'.

a Find an example of the imperative in the text.

b If the writer used more imperatives, how would this change the feel of the advice?

Word level focus

1 The words in this chart all appear in the text. Think about the patterns and fill in the missing words.

Present tense	Present participle	Noun
revise	revising	revision
distract	distracting	distraction
concentrate		concentration
		meditation

Writing advice

Imagine that you are an advice columnist in a teenage magazine.
You receive this letter. What advice would you give?

Dear Sophie,

I've got a group of friends who I've known for years. We all went to the same primary school and now go to the same high school. Each week we go to the youth club and I'm beginning to hate it. They all have new outfits each week, have strings of boys after them and chat for hours to each other on their mobile phones. My parents can't afford to buy me new clothes as often as my mates and they'd never agree to a mobile. I'm beginning to feel like the odd one out. I can't tell mum or dad as they'd feel awful that I'm left out. Any help?

Kelly, 14

Planning

- Look at the problems and think about what advice you could give.
- Try to be practical and sympathetic – don't give silly answers.

Advice on structure and language

- Try to keep your advice short and to the point.
- Keep your tone friendly and positive.

Drafting

- Avoid the imperative – you are giving advice, not instructions.
- Make sure that you reassure your reader.
- Try to link your paragraphs so your advice flows in a logical way.

Revising

- Get a friend to read it. What do they like? What would they change?
- Is the tone of your advice friendly and right for your reader?

Do you ever write letters to friends or family? What about emails? Have you ever written an official letter? You might not write actual letters very often, because telephones, e-mail and faxes have provided easier and faster ways to communicate. But you will be expected to write letters for jobs and courses in the future so it's important to know how to write them properly.

For hundreds of years, letters have been an important way for people to communicate. They tend to fall into two main styles – formal and informal.

 Exploring letters

Look at these two letters. See what differences you notice in:

a the layout of each letter

b how the reader is addressed

c the sort of language used

d the tone (is it polite or chatty, for example?)

e the endings.

Formal

Heaven Holidays

Heaven Holidays PLC
Westlake House
Norton Street
Bury St. Edmunds
IP33 4AB

20 July 2000

Mr. S. Goodes
34 Lime Road
Warwick
CV23 2ES

Dear Mr. Goodes,
Heaven Holidays Booking Confirmation

I am writing to confirm receipt of your letter and deposit cheque dated 12 July 2000. Please find enclosed a receipt and brochure giving further details of the holiday property that you have selected.

May I remind you that the remainder of payment is due 6 weeks before the holiday commences. Should you need any assistance in the meantime, please do not hesitate to contact me at the address above.

Yours faithfully

Jackie Fitzgerald (customer services division)

47 Kirkby Road
Harrogate
HG2 9YZ
20 July 2000

Dear Toni,

Thanks a lot for the card and present. It'll be really handy when we go on our hols later this summer. You going anywhere?

This is just a shortie 'cos we're going swimming and then to the pics to see Chicken Run. With a bit of luck, dad'll take us for some scram from McDonalds - a proper day out!

See you soon,

Ali

Letters are also written to suit a specific audience and for a purpose. So the writer has to use appropriate language and a suitable style.

Look at these extracts from letters and for each one decide:

- who its audience is (do the reader and writer know each other or not?)
- what its purpose is (is it social, to inform someone of something, etc.?)
- whether it's formal or informal (does it use slang? are the sentences complete? is the tone serious or friendly?)

1

Thank you for attending an interview yesterday at Oxford University Press. It is with great pleasure that I confirm your appointment as....

2

Ta for your last letter. Great to hear from you. You studying for exams?

3

I wish to complain about the late running buses to Ipswich. On two occasions within the last week I have been late for important appointments.

4

Would you mind doing me a big favour? I wouldn't ask but you are a mate. Could I borrow some of the gear that you wore for Heidi's wedding?

5

Your money can help other animals like Charlie receive the expert care and attention that they deserve. Send your donation to us now. We'll be waiting for your reply.

The key to writing letters

Formal

Your address

Date

Name of recipient
Address of recipient

Dear Mr Ms or Miss (if you know their name)
Dear Sir or Madam (if you don't)

Write the letter
use formal language (no slang)
write in complete sentences

Yours faithfully
(if you don't know the person well)
Yours sincerely
(if you do know the person well)

Your name (including surname)

Informal

Your address

Date

Dear _____ (usually first name)

Write the letter

use informal language
use slang if you like
use incomplete sentences if you like

An informal and friendly ending, e.g.
Cheers
See you soon
TTFN
Catch you later

Your name (first name only)

Obviously as times have changed so has the English language, and letters now sound less formal than in the past. The first three letters you will be looking at in this unit are informal ones, one of which was written in the past.

Letter from Murray Duffin, Royal Navy

Murray Duffin served on board HMS Arrow during the Falklands War in 1982. He sent this letter from his ship in the South Atlantic to his family in England.

4 Mess

HMS Arrow

6/5/82

Dear All

I got mailys from you today dated 16–20 April. Thanks very much, they cheered me up no end and believe me I needed it as yesterday was pretty terrible.

At 1400 we went to action stations due to an air threat and straight after [wards] Sheffield was hit by an Exocet fired from an aircraft. As I've told you, this is a devastating missile and one alone can sink a ship. We were the nearest and we went to her aid. As we closed in a sub fired two torpedoes at us. We managed to avoid them both by some skillful manouvering. We went in and after some valiant efforts to save the ship she had to be abandoned as they thought the Sea-Dart mag was going to blow and that would have taken us as well.

I was busy with the torpedoes as we were attacking the sub. Some debris was spotted but we're unsure as to whether it was sunk or not.

When I was not prepping torps I was helping with the casualties which were in the hanger. It wasn't very nice and there are some things I pray I'll never see again.

We took off about 220 and kept them overnight, we all gave up our pits but I only had 0200 to 0600 off during the whole day anyway so I slept on station as it wasn't worth leaving.

I know this isn't much of an account but I don't really want to write it all out... The death toll is estimated at 20–30 but I haven't heard any definite reports.

One side of our ship is all battered where we were bouncing off the Sheffield. In fact Arrow's looking pretty sorry for herself altogether what with the punishment we've been taking. I expect once we turn for home we'll work harder than ever painting and cleaning so she looks good for when we get in. Me and Debbie [a crewman] were both told that they were very pleased with the way we worked and it was noted that we were always there to lend a hand – it's nice to be appreciated for a change.

Anyway let's hope that's the first and last time that happens... I think it's a good idea, transferring my money into a Deposit Account so ta very much. As to me needing anything – actually there isn't.

I got four letters from the girl in Guzz – her name's Kerry and she sent me her gold cross and chain to wear as she thought it would protect me and remind me of her. She's being great with letters and stuff so that's nice... Anyway folks that's about all. I'm well and in good spirits and the morale aboard is high, especially now that we've had a mail drop. I don't think it could have come at a better time – ie the day after Sheffield got hit.

I've just heard that she's still floating; when we left her she was engulfed in flames and the intention was to sink her with gunfire but then another air attack came and we left rather smartish so I don't know what will happen to her now.

I'm glad everythings ok at home and the pennies are rolling in. Don't worry about me. I'll be ok

lots of love

Murray

Word bank

pits beds   **prepping torps** preparing torpedoes for launch
Sea-Dart mag the chamber for firing Sea-Dart sea-to-air missiles

Text level focus

1 Why was this letter written (what is its purpose)?

2 Every text has an audience. Who is the audience of this text? How can you tell?

3 Look at the layout features of the letter. Which things tell you that it is informal?

4 What impression do you get of the writer from his letter? Look at the suggestions below to help you but add ideas of your own too. Try to say why you get these impressions.
   - cheerful • positive • unhappy
   - confident • brave

Sentence level focus

1 Letters like this one can use informal sentences, which sound rather like conversation. Find two examples of these sentences here. Can you say why the writer uses this informal style?

2 This is an informal, personal letter in which the writer expresses how he feels. Look at this sentence:

When I was not prepping torps I was helping with the casualties which were in the hanger. It wasn't very nice and there are some things I pray I'll never see again.

What would happen if you made it more formal and impersonal? Try changing 'I' to 'he' and making the words more formal. How does the tone and style change?

3 One informal feature of this writer's style is how little punctuation he uses. Look at this sentence where the writer has not used any commas:

In fact Arrow's looking pretty sorry for herself altogether what with the punishment we've been taking.

If he had added commas to break it up, it might look like this:

In fact, Arrow's looking pretty sorry for herself altogether, what with the punishment we've been taking.

Read it aloud to yourself – you should see that it is easier to follow.

Now look at these sentences and add commas to make them read better.

a *Thanks very much, they cheered me up no end and believe me I needed it as yesterday was pretty terrible.*

b *When we left her she was engulfed in flames and the intention was to sink her with gunfire but then another air attack came and we left rather smartish so I don't know what will happen to her now.*

> Remember, commas are used:
> - to add pauses in a sentence
> - to separate clauses.

Word level focus

1 Because this is a personal letter, the writer's style is informal. Pick out examples of informal language. The hints below will help you:

- look at how the date is written
- look at how he starts and signs off the letter
- look at the vocabulary – is it formal or chatty?

2 The letter uses a mixture of formal and informal language. Look at these examples and sort them out into the right column of the chart.

Formal	Informal

mailys   devastating
went to her aid   sub
death toll   ta
smartish   engulfed
ok   pennies rolling in
transferring   intention

Letter from Charlotte Brontë

Charlotte Brontë was one of the famous Brontë sisters. Her novels include *Jane Eyre* and *Shirley*. *Jane Eyre* is based upon her experiences as a governess (a sort of nanny and live-in teacher). She wrote this letter to her sister Emily – but she calls her Lavinia at the beginning, as a sort of pet name. You will notice that the style is formal even though it is a letter between sisters.

The letter includes a lot of old-fashioned words, which are not explained: there is an activity to help you work out what they mean.

8th June 1839

Dearest Lavinia,

I am most exceedingly obliged to you for the trouble you have taken in seeking up my things and sending them all right. The box and its contents were most acceptable. I only wish I had asked you to send me some letter-paper. This is my last sheet but two. When you can send the other articles of raiment now manufacturing, I shall be right down glad of them.

I have striven hard to be pleased with my new situation. The country, the house, and the grounds are, as I have said, divine. But, alack-a-day! there is such a thing as seeing all beautiful around you – pleasant woods, winding white paths, green lawns, and blue sunshiny sky – and not having a free moment or a free thought left to enjoy them in. The children are constantly with me, and more riotous, perverse, unmanageable cubs never grew. As for correcting them, I soon quickly found that was entirely out of the question: they are to do as they like. A complaint to Mrs Sidgwick brings only black looks upon oneself, and unjust, partial excuses to screen the children. I have tried that plan once. It succeeded so notably that I shall try it no more. I said in my last letter that Mrs Sidgwick did not know me. I now begin to find that she does not intend to know me, that she cares nothing in the world about me except to contrive how the greatest possible quantity of labour may be squeezed out of me, and to that end she overwhelms me with oceans of needlework, yards of cambric to hem, muslin nightcaps to make, and, above all things, dolls to dress. I do not think she likes me at all, because I can't help being shy in such an entirely novel scene, surrounded as I have hitherto been by strange and constantly changing faces. I used to think I should like to be in the stir of grand folks' society but I have had enough of it – it is dreary work to look on and listen. I see now more clearly than I have ever done before that a private governess has no existence, is not considered as a living and rational being except as connected with the wearisome duties she has to fulfil. While she is teaching the children, working for them, amusing them, it is all right. If she steals a moment for herself she is a nuisance. Nevertheless, Mrs Sidgwick is universally considered an amiable woman. Her manners are fussily affable. She talks a great deal, but as it seems to me not much to the purpose. Perhaps I may like her better after a while. At present I have no call to her. Mr Sidgwick is in my opinion a hundred times better – less profession, less bustling condescension, but a far kinder heart. It is very seldom that he speaks to me, but when he does I always feel happier and more settled for some minutes after. He never asks me to wipe the children's smutty noses or tie their shoes or fetch their pinafores or set them a chair. One of the pleasantest afternoons I have spent here – indeed, the only one at all pleasant – was when Mr Sidgwick walked out with his children, and I had orders to follow a little behind. As he strolled on through his fields with his magnificent Newfoundland dog at his side, he looked very like what a frank, wealthy, Conservative gentleman ought to be. He spoke freely and unaffectedly to the people he met, and though he indulged his children and allowed them to tease himself far too much, he would not suffer them grossly to insult others.

Text level focus

1 Pick out two features which show that this is a letter.

2 What would you say is the purpose of this text?

3 What impressions does Charlotte Brontë give of her situation? Use the prompts on the right to help you answer.

- What does she think about her new job?
- What does she think about the children?
- Why does she like Mr Sidgwick but not his wife?

Back up your points with examples from the letter.

Sentence level focus

1 Which tense does the writer mainly use? Explain why.

2 The writer uses all three sentence types in this letter.

Look at these examples and decide which sentence type is being used:

a When you can send the other articles of raiment now manufacturing, I shall be right down glad of them.

b I have tried that plan once.

c Perhaps I may like her better after a while.

d It is very seldom that he speaks to me, but when he does I always feel happier and more settled for some minutes after.

e As he strolled on through his fields with his magnificent Newfoundland dog at his side, he looked very like what a frank, wealthy, Conservative gentleman ought to be.

Now explain how you know which type of sentence is which.

> Simple sentences contain one idea, e.g.
> I went to visit my aunt.
>
> Compound sentences contain two or more ideas joined by 'and', 'but', or 'or', e.g.
> I went to visit my aunt, but she wasn't in.
>
> Complex sentences are made up of a main clause (which would make sense on its own) and one or more subordinate clauses (which add more information but could not stand alone) e.g.
> I visited my aunt, who lives in New York.
>
> main clause   subordinate clause
> (works on its own)   (more information, but doesn't work on its own)

Word level focus

1 This letter uses some words which we no longer use today (or at least not very often). Try to match up each word with a word we might use today (looking at the way the words are used in the letter will help you to match up some of them; for others you might need to use a dictionary).

raiment	job
striven	being made
situation	tried
hitherto	clothes
manufacturing	up to now
perverse	honest
affable	being made
frank	friendly

E-mail

E-mail is probably the fastest-growing kind of communication. We can send messages from one computer to another in a few seconds – or even from a computer to a mobile phone. E-mail does not look quite like letters on paper, and has its own peculiarities of style.

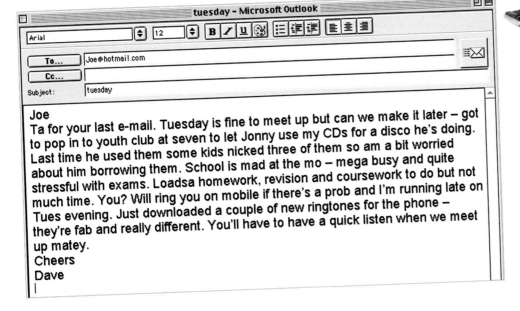

tuesday – Microsoft Outlook

To... | Joe@hotmail.com

Cc...

Subject: | tuesday

Joe
Ta for your last e-mail. Tuesday is fine to meet up but can we make it later – got to pop in to youth club at seven to let Jonny use my CDs for a disco he's doing. Last time he used them some kids nicked three of them so am a bit worried about him borrowing them. School is mad at the mo – mega busy and quite stressful with exams. Loadsa homework, revision and coursework to do but not much time. You? Will ring you on mobile if there's a prob and I'm running late on Tues evening. Just downloaded a couple of new ringtones for the phone – they're fab and really different. You'll have to have a quick listen when we meet up matey.
Cheers
Dave

Text level focus

1 How can you tell that this is an e-mail? Look specifically at the text.

2 The writer has not used paragraphs here because it is an informal and chatty style of writing and between two friends. Where would you divide the text into paragraphs?

Sentence level focus

1 Look at the sentence structures in the e-mail.

   a Are they formal or informal? Are they long or short? Are they all complete sentences?

   b What would happen if you rewrote the e-mail in complete sentences? Would the tone alter?

Word level focus

1 E-mails like this use relaxed and casual language in the email. Pick out three examples of this. Why do you think the writer has not used more formal language here?

Writing an informal letter

Write a letter to a friend explaining what you did in the last school holidays.

Research and planning

- Think about things you did that would be interesting for the reader.

Advice on structure and language

- Set it out informally – look back at *The key to writing letters*.

- Remember your audience – keep it friendly and relaxed.

- Try to use a range of sentence types – simple and compound sentences are the least formal.

- You can use language that might not be acceptable in formal writing – such as 'cool'.

Drafting

- Get your ideas down on paper and then be prepared to rework parts.

Revising

- Get a friend to check your work and see if the language and structure are suitable for your audience.

Formal letter of complaint

This letter was sent to a holiday company about a holiday that did not turn out as expected. Before you read it and study it in detail, look back at *Exploring letters* and remind yourself of the features of a formal letter.

Leafy Brook
179 Dingle Meadows
Great Haughley
20th July 2000

The Managing Director
Frank Lee Orval Holidays PLC
22-28 Great Farnham Street
London
N34 5FT

Dear Sir/Madam,

Further to our telephone conversation on 20th July 2000, I am writing to express my dissatisfaction with our recent holiday, booked through your company.

Firstly, the tickets, which were supposed to arrive at your agency two weeks prior to departure, failed to arrive. This meant endless telephone calls with your staff who, although helpful, did not get the tickets to me until the day before we departed.

Next, the plane was overbooked and my husband and I were asked if we would be prepared to take a later flight. We appreciate that this can occasionally happen but it did mean that we would miss a day of our holiday. The hotel near the airport was very comfortable and we were transported there in style – but it was not Greece! I think that if people book holidays in good faith then the tour operator should ensure that they can provide what people book.

To add insult to injury, on arrival at our destination (by now our 14 night holiday had been cut to 13) we discovered that half of the hotel was still being constructed. To be greeted by a queue of juggernauts and a building site atmosphere was the last thing we expected. In no way did your brochure indicate that this was the situation. Had it been made clear, I would not have booked it and in this instance I think serious compensation should be awarded.

Furthermore, the workmen began work each day at 6.30 am. This meant that the noise made it impossible to sleep. The hotel manager was unsympathetic and pointed out that the reduced price of the holiday should have been an indication of a less than 5* hotel. However, this was not made clear to us or any of the other residents at the hotel.

Your brochure states 'only a hop, skip and a jump from the beach and other facilities'. All I can say is that it must be a hop, skip and a jump for a giant. We are in our mid-thirties so young, fit and healthy but it took us at least 15 minutes to reach the beach.

To sum up, while I would have put up with the late tickets and the overbooked plane, our entire holiday has been ruined. I feel that we have been misled, misinformed and taken for fools, to put it frankly. I would appreciate a swift reply, with details of what compensation you are going to offer us.

Yours faithfully,

Nicola Swift (Mrs)

Text level focus

1   What features tell you that this is a formal letter?

2   The opening paragraph of a formal letter should say what the letter will be about. Look at this paragraph. What is the subject of this letter?

3   Paragraphs often start by stating a fact, and then expand upon that fact. Look at paragraphs 2–5. What is the fact in each one, and how does the writer elaborate on it?

4   The final paragraph should draw a formal letter together. How does the writer do this in her final paragraph?

5   How would you describe the writer's style in this letter?

- direct and controlled
- angry
- rude and bad mannered
- chatty and informal

Explain your ideas with a careful choice of examples from the letter.

Sentence level focus

1 There are several compound sentences in the letter. Look at this example:

Next, the plane was overbooked and my husband and I were asked if we would be prepared to take a later flight.

This could also be expressed as a complex sentence, which might look something like this:

Next, because the plane was overbooked, my husband and I were asked if we would be prepared to take a later flight.

It now sounds more formal and serious (which shows that the writer means business).

The list below shows you some of the words used in complex sentences. Rework these two compound sentences as complex sentences.

a *The hotel near the airport was very comfortable and we were transported there in style but it was not Greece!*

b *We are in our mid-thirties so young, fit and healthy but it took us at least 15 minutes to reach the beach.*

Who	When	Even though	If
Though	Until	Where	As
Since	Although	Before	Because

> A compound sentence contains two or more ideas joined by 'and' 'but' and 'or'.
>
> *We went to the beach and played in the sea.*
>
> A complex sentence is made up of a main clause (which would make sense on its own) and one or more subordinate clauses (which add more information but could not stand alone) e.g.
>
> *We went to the beach which is four miles from the house.*
>
> main clause   subordinate clause
> (works on its own)   (more information, but doesn't work on its own)

2 Occasionally the writer uses a simple sentence. Look at the opening to paragraph 5. Why do you think she has used a simple sentence here?

3 Discourse markers can be used to guide the reader through a formal letter. List the discourse markers the writer uses, and then suggest alternatives she could have used.

> Discourse markers are words and phrases which link a text together and help the reader follow how the text is developing, e.g. 'firstly', 'then', 'finally'.

Word level focus

1 Much of the language in the letter is formal.

a Look at these words and think of an informal word to replace the formal one:

- I am writing to express my dissatisfaction
- We appreciate that this can occasionally happen
- we discovered that half of the hotel was still being constructed.
- The hotel manager was unsympathetic

b Now look at your new versions. Do the sentences sound as if they should be taken as seriously as the old versions?

What would you send?

Writing a formal letter

Write a letter to your local council complaining that there are not enough facilities for young people where you live and making suggestions for improvements.

Research and planning

- Think about what there is to do at present in the area (you'll have to suggest that this is not enough, so young people are missing out).

- Try to think of new ideas that could be suitable (e.g. skateboard park, cyber café) and how these might help young people.

- Focus on your 3-4 best points.

- Decide on a suitable order for your points.

- Remember that you have to convince the local council to take you seriously so make positive suggestions, don't just moan on and on.

Advice on structure and language

- Set it out formally – look back at *The key to writing letters*.

- Have a definite structure – introduction (saying what the letter is about), main part, then ending (drawing your letter together).

- Try to use complex sentences, to make your writing sound serious and adult.

- Use formal vocabulary to set the right tone.

- Start a new paragraph for each new idea.

Drafting

- Get your ideas down on paper and then be prepared to rework parts.

- Keep it polite and professional.

Revising

- Does it sound formal enough?

- Does the reader gain some understanding of what your problem is and what you require?

Facts, facts, facts

How many different sorts of texts can you think of which retell facts?

- Information texts can put across facts about a wide variety of subjects.

- A biography tells the facts about someone's life.

- Reports are often written from first-hand experience, and range from news reports to the reports in a school newsletter.

You will be looking at all these kinds of texts in this unit.

 # Exploring information texts

Look at these extracts from information texts. The first one is aimed at adults and the second one at children.

Children and asthma

Asthma is caused when the air passages in the lungs become narrowed, making it difficult to breathe. It is the sudden narrowing of the air passages which causes an attack. This can usually be relieved by using an inhaler. It is important when this happens that the child breathes slowly and deeply and is kept calm. However, in extreme cases, when the child becomes exhausted or distressed, hospital treatment may be necessary.

Shark attack

Most sharks are not dangerous and leave people alone. Sharks attack about 50 to 75 people each year in the world, but only 5 to 10 of these reported attacks result in death. People are more likely to die in car accidents or drown in the sea than be killed by a shark. Attacks may occur when a shark mistakes a person for its normal prey, biting a foot that looks like a fish. A shark may attack if it feels threatened or is provoked. It is dangerous to be in water where there may be sharks: if the water is murky, if you have cut yourself, or if bait has been put out for fish. Always take advice if there are sharks in the area – never swim alone or at night.

Now think about how the texts have been written:

a What tense is used?

b What does the first sentence of each text do?

c Do the texts use language that appeals to your emotions?

d Which person of the verb (this means 'I', 'you', 'he/she/it', 'we' or 'they') is used in each text?

e Do they feel easy or difficult to read? Are the sentences long or short? How does this relate to the audience for each text?

 # The key to writing information texts

To write an information text you should:

- write in the present tense because you are trying to put across current information

- open with a general statement about the topic ('Asthma is caused when…' 'Most sharks are not dangerous')

- write in the third person ('it', 'the child', 'sharks')

- provide comparisons to illustrate your points or put information in context ('People are more likely to die in car accidents or drown in the sea than be killed by a shark')

- concentrate on facts, not opinions – so do not use emotive language

- write in the sort of sentences which are suitable for your audience.

RSPCA information leaflet

This information is from the RSPCA to teach the public about baby foxes, and why they should not be 'rescued' from the wild.

RSPCA **Information**

All alone?

If you see a fox club by itself please think twice before you 'rescue' it. You may be doing more harm than good.

RSPCA

Not alone

In the spring and early summer RSPCA wildlife hospitals and animal centres have to deal with hundreds of fox cubs brought in by well-meaning people who think these appealing animals have been abandoned or orphaned.

In reality these cubs usually have parents or close relatives quite near by. Fox cubs start to leave the earth – their home – when they are about four weeks old. It is quite a normal part of a fox's growing up process to spend its days alone in or around patches of cover above ground.

At risk

RSPCA research shows that fox cubs taken from the wild, treated and rehabilitated – even with the best of care – are less likely to survive when they return to their natural habitat than completely wild foxes. This is because they don't have a chance to develop their survival and hunting skills. Fox cubs learn these skills while exploring the area around their home. Rehabilitated fox cubs wander a lot further afield than their fully wild counterparts and so are often killed on the roads.

▲ A four-week-old cub is usually a dark chocolate brown colour, with a short, puppy-like face, short ears and blue eyes.

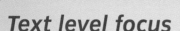

Text level focus

1 Which of these presentational devices have been used in the leaflet?

- headline
- pictures
- logo
- coloured panels
- large fonts
- short paragraphs
- borders
- subheadings
- captions
- bullet points

2 Information texts usually start with a sentence to introduce the topic. Read the sentences on the front of the leaflet. How do they do this?

3 What tense is this text written in? Why?

4 The first sentence in a newspaper report should answer these five questions (the 'five Ws'): who, what, where, when, why. Can you find answers to these questions in the first paragraph on page 2 of the leaflet?

5 Information texts focus on facts, not opinions. Find three facts in the second paragraph on this page. Are there any opinions here?

6 Texts like this use comparisons to make their information clearer. Can you find a comparison in the caption on page 2 of the leaflet? How does it help the reader?

Sentence level focus

1 In the caption on the front of the leaflet, the writer uses the pronoun 'you' to address the reader. What effect does this have?

- It makes the text more personal and friendly.
- It tries to give the reader advice and suggestions in a relaxed way.
- It makes the reader feel important.
- It shows the leaflet was written for one particular person.

2 Many information texts are written in the third person (using 'he/she/it/they'). Can you find any element of this here?

Word level focus

1 The text uses some fairly technical language connected to its topic. Find these words in the text. Which of the words in the second group means the same?

abandoned	fellows
orphaned	home
rehabilitated	without parents
habitat	away
afield	deserted
counterparts	put back to normal

2 Look at the front cover again. Why has the writer put the word 'rescue' in inverted commas?

Writing an information text

Design an information sheet for new students coming to your school in September.

Research and planning

- Decide on the areas that you think they'll want information on – school dinners, clubs in the lunch hour or after school, what subjects are studied, etc.

- Decide how to present the information for easy use – think about what headings to use. Will you use bullet points, pictures, etc.?

Advice on structure and language

- Remember to use subheadings for the different areas you cover.

- Use the present tense.

- Be positive – don't scare them off!

- Keep your language level suitable for your audience.

Drafting

- Make sure that the layout is clear – this will help your reader find the information they want.

- Make sure your style is friendly and informative – give them facts.

Revising

- Does your sheet give an overview of the school and what new students can expect?

- Does it look right – would a future student want to read it?

Exploring biography

Biographies retell facts from someone else's life. Look at these extracts to find out more about what makes biographies special.

A

Dawn French by Alison Bowyer

On graduating from Central, Dawn excitedly took up her teaching post at the Parliament Hill School for Girls, in Highgate. The day she arrived at the school was an important one for Dawn. She had dreamed of becoming a teacher ever since she was a thirteen-year-old girl in Miss Abbott's class at St. Dunstan's Abbey, and now the dream had become a reality. She had no idea that teaching was not in fact where her future lay, and she threw herself into her new job.

B

Rowan Atkinson by Bruce Dessau

Beyond the school gates his interests had always veered towards the scientific. At home and on the farm he would spend hours tinkering with machinery and polishing tractors. He could barely wait until he was old enough to drive them. Eventually he got his first taste of speed behind the wheel, and while it might not have been up to Grand Prix standards, even 18mph can feel like 180mph when you are the person with your foot on the tractor's accelerator. Even before he was old enough to take his driving test he had learnt about motor mechanics by taking apart his mother's old Morris Minor, which she didn't want any more.

C

Princess Diana by Richard Wood

However awful Diana felt privately, she knew that 'the show must go on'. She quickly learned to cover up her inner feelings with an amazing show of happiness. The press loved her. She was treated like a film star. Diana was the most photographed woman in the world.

At times, all this attention became too much for Diana. She tried to persuade photographers not to pursue her. When that did not work, she tried to shake them off, slipping out of back doors, hiding her face behind bags, and driving off at speed. But Diana knew that she could never entirely escape their attention.

After reading the three texts, look at these questions in small groups:

- What is the purpose of each text?

- Are specific people or individuals the focus of the texts?

- What impression do you get of the person each text is about?

- Do the extracts tell their events in the order they happened (chronological order)? Do they use flashbacks at all? (A flashback takes the reader back to an earlier event to help us understand more of what is happening now.)

- What words and phrases do the writers use to show the order things happened? (These words and phrases are called temporal markers.)

- Which tense is used in each extract? Why?

- What person of the verb is used ('I', 'you', 'he/she/it')?

You probably noticed that:

- The texts all try to provide information about their subject, and tell facts about different times in their life – for example, text A is about Dawn French's years as a teacher.

- They all focus on a particular individual: Dawn French, Rowan Atkinson, and Diana, Princess of Wales.

- Each text gives a different impression of the person it is about. For instance, text C suggests that Diana was brave, covering up her 'inner feelings' although she hated all the media attention she got. Texts A and B are about more positive parts of their subjects' lives.

- Text A is in chronological order, taking Dawn French from graduation to work as a teacher – it does use a flashback to tell us about her long-standing ambition to teach. The order of texts B and C is vague, as they deal with more general information rather than a specific sequence of time.

- All the texts use temporal markers to some extent: text C 'at times', text B 'even before he was old enough'.

- They are all written in the past tense, as the events described in them have already happened.

- They are all written in the third person ('he/she').

⚷ **The key to writing biography**

If you are writing a biography, you should:

- aim to inform about a person, retell facts from their life, and perhaps entertain the reader

- write in the past tense

- write in the third person ('he/she')

- focus on one individual and tell the story from their point of view

- use temporal markers ('ever since…', 'eventually') to show shifts in time

- tell the story roughly in chronological order, sometimes using flashbacks to fill in extra information

- aim to give a strong impression of the subject's character.

Anne Frank

Anne Frank's diary has been translated into many languages. It is seen as one of the most important pieces of personal writing about World War II, and Anne's life story has become important because of her diary. This extract is from a biography of Anne.

Anne Frank – The Biography

In her tiny new cage, each day was like the next, and although she had time enough to experience her feelings, there was no space. She couldn't scream, sing, or cry when she wanted. She had to learn to express her feelings only at certain times, an ability even adults acquire only with age. When the bathroom was unoccupied, she would hide there and weep from loneliness. 'I can't refrain from telling you that lately I have begun to feel deserted. I am surrounded by too great a void,' Anne wrote in her diary on November 20, three and a half months after she had gone into hiding. 'I never used to feel like this, my fun and amusements, my girlfriends, completely filled my thoughts. Now I either think about unhappy things, or about myself' (ver. B).

The diary had been the first thing Anne packed in her school-bag on the hectic last evening at home, as if she already knew what an important role it would play in her life. Two months would pass in the annex, however, before Anne began to write in it regularly. Until then, she had managed to record something only every few weeks; her new situation claimed all her attention. But toward the end of September 1942 she had the idea of treating her entries as letters: 'I would just love to correspond with somebody, so that is what I intend to do in future with my diary. I shall write it from now on in letter form, which actually comes to the same thing' (Sept. 21; ver. A). Anne wrote this entry with her fountain pen, a gift she had received on her ninth birthday from her grandmother in Aachen (her fingers, friends recalled, seemed always to be stained a grayish blue thereafter). Unlike her later entries, which she wrote in a fluent, confident cursive, this one is printed in the rounded letters of a child's hand.

From then on, Anne wrote in her diary almost every day. Holding her pen in her own particular fashion between her index and middle fingers, she wrote to Jettje or Emmy, to Pop or Marianne, to Pien, Conny, or Kitty. To these imaginary friends, she wrote long letters chronicling everyday life in the secret annex. With them, she could laugh, cry, forget her isolation. Here and there she pasted photos of herself and her friends in among her letters, adding captions that were critical but always humorous.

Text level focus

1 To make the order of events clear, biographies use temporal markers (phrases that give an idea of time such as 'to begin with'). Find three examples of temporal markers in the text.

2 What impression do you form of Anne Frank from this extract?

- She is fed up and lonely.
- She has very little to amuse her.
- She tries hard to keep her sense of humour.

Remember to give examples from the extract to back up your opinions.

3 This text uses Anne Frank's diary but it is not all written from her point of view. How reliable do you think it is in helping the reader form an impression of Anne?

- very reliable
- not very reliable   • not at all reliable

Say why you have chosen your answer.

4 Biography writers sometimes use flashbacks. For example:

Anne wrote this entry with her fountain pen, a gift she had received on her ninth birthday from her grandmother in Aachen (her fingers, friends recalled, seemed always to be stained a grayish blue thereafter).

a Find another example of a use of flashback in the passage.

b Why do you think the writer does this?

- to give information about Anne's life before she went into hiding
- because the writer can't remember what she has said already
- to stress how important the diary and writing in it would become to Anne
- to show how Anne had plenty of time to think back to her life before.

Try to give reasons for your choices.

Sentence level focus

1 What tense does the writer use in this text?

2 Biographies are normally written in the third person. Find an example of the pronoun used.

3 Complex sentences can be used in biographies to build up detail, e.g.

When the bathroom was unoccupied, she would hide there and weep from loneliness.

Main clause –
she would hide there and weep from loneliness

Subordinate clause –
When the bathroom was unoccupied

The two clauses are separated with a comma.

Look at these examples and decide whether they are complex sentences using the following guide:

- Does the sentence fall into two or more parts?
- Is there a comma used to separate clauses?
- Would the main clause make sense on its own, but not the subordinate clause?

a She had to learn to express her feelings only at certain times, an ability even adults acquire only with age.

b The diary had been the first thing Anne had packed in her school-bag on the hectic last evening at home, as if she already knew what an important role it would play in her life.

c Two months would pass in the annex, however, before Anne began to write in it regularly.

d 'I shall write it in letter form, which actually comes to the same thing.'

Complex sentences are made up of a main clause (which would make sense on its own) and one or more subordinate clauses (which add more information but could not stand alone) e.g.

Biography is about people who are interesting.

main clause (works on its own)

subordinate clause (more information, but doesn't work on its own)

Word level focus

1 Texts focusing on people's lives will use words relating to thoughts, feelings and descriptions. Look at these examples from the text and place the highlighted words in the correct column of the chart.

Thoughts and feelings (things that are personal)	Descriptions (of places, people and things, etc.)

- When the bathroom was unoccupied, she would hide there and weep from loneliness.
- The diary had been the first thing Anne packed in her school-bag on the hectic last evening at home
- With them, she could laugh, cry, forget her isolation.
- She wrote long letters chronicling everyday life in the secret annexe

Explain, in your own words, why the writer needs to give some indication of thoughts, feelings and description.

2 Biographies have to put across how their subject felt about things. One way of doing this is by using emotionally-charged vocabulary.

a Look at this list of words and decide which words are emotive.

scream	sing
cage	correspond
cry	unoccupied
weep	attention
void	isolation

b Then for the ones that you think are emotive, explain what impression they give us of how Anne might have felt in the secret annex. For example, 'cage' suggests that she felt she was imprisoned like an animal.

Writing a biography

Write a biographical piece about a favourite character – a real person, or someone from a television programme, film or book.

Research and planning

- Select your person.
- Find out more about this person if you need to.
- Choose a key time or point in their life to focus on.
- Plan your outline in paragraphs – keep it short and to the point.

Advice on structure and language

- Use the third person singular ('he/she/it') or plural ('they').
- Use the past tense.
- Use temporal markers to make it clear what order things happened in.
- Try to let the reader know how your subject might have felt: use emotive vocabulary for this.
- Use complex sentences to build up detail.
- Keep your style formal.

Drafting

- Try not to say too much – keep the pace and flow going.
- Don't be afraid of editing or moving bits to other points – don't forget you can use flashbacks.
- Check that your style is lively but formal.

Revising

- Read it to a friend and ask them what they would change.

Exploring reports

We find reports everywhere in everyday life – in newspapers, school work, school reports, on television, on the radio, etc. Reports are factual pieces of writing, often written from first-hand experiences.

Look at these two reports – they are written in quite different styles.

A Extract from a School report

School news

Friday. The best day of the week or at least it would be this week as we were going to the Millennium Dome. It was the chance of a lifetime as we'd been told that the Dome was only open for a year.

On arrival, we were promptly tagged and let loose to be back by 6pm at the coach. Our first port of call was the Sky news studio where we queued for an eternity to have the chance of reading the news and getting a free copy of our efforts on tape. The atmosphere in the studio was electric as hundreds of kids waited excitedly for their turn. When it came to it, I found it hard to read with a straight face with so many people watching me.

B

Television news report

One of the world-famous Concorde planes caught on fire as it departed from Charles De Gaulle airport in Paris, this afternoon. Onlookers said they were 'horrified' to witness the plane turning into a ball of fire as it left the runway. Within minutes, the plane crash-landed and debris spilled over the suburbs of Paris, killing holidaymakers in a local hotel. It is believed that the plane, en route for New York, was carrying German passengers who had transferred at Paris for the Atlantic crossing. It may take several days before the cause of the disaster can be established.

Now answer these questions about the two reports:

a Which tense is used in each text?

b What sort of order do the texts report their events in?

c Do the texts open with a sentence which sums up the information that will follow? (This is called a topic sentence.)

d Do the writers use temporal markers? (These are words which show the order things happened in: 'at 6 o'clock', 'yesterday evening', 'by then', 'until now'.)

e Which text is more personal and lively?

f Which text is more impersonal and factual?

g What would be the effect if the writer of text B gave their opinion, as in text A?

 The key to writing reports

When you are writing a report you should:

- use the past tense, as the events being described have already happened
- write in chronological order (in sequence)
- use temporal markers showing this
- make your writing personal and lively, if you are reporting an event from your own point of view
- make your writing impersonal and more factual, if you are reporting an event for the news.

BBC World Service Radio News

This report was broadcast on the BBC World Service, a radio station that can be listened to throughout the world. The broadcasts cover international news rather than national news in the UK. This report was broadcast at midday on Sunday July 2, 2000.

News transcript

Announcer   Ten survivors of an Indonesian ferry, which sank with heavy loss of life, have been picked up at sea after clinging to debris for more than three days. The group, part of a large number of Christians fleeing religious violence, confirmed reports that the ferry sank three days ago in rough seas. Jonathon Head reports from Jakarta.

Reporter   After three days of searching for the missing ferry, the discovery of survivors has at last confirmed its fate. The ten people plucked from the sea had been clinging to debris for three days and had drifted north to Indonesia's border with the Philippines. They said the ferry had sunk in heavy seas on Thursday, probably a short time after the last emergency radio call from the captain when he said his engines had failed and the ship was taking in water. Four Indonesian Navy ships backed by fishing boats and navy patrol aircraft are continuing the search for other survivors in the area but rescue officials believe the chances of finding anyone else alive after so long in the sea are slim.

Text level focus

1 How is the report structured? Look at what the announcer says and what the reporter says afterwards.

2 News reports are highly factual. Pick out three examples of facts in this text.

3 No interviews or quotations are used in the report whereas most television and newspaper reports include this. How does the reporter tell us simple information from the survivors' point of view?

4 Look at this sentence from the report. The style here is factual and impersonal (the reporter does not say what he or she thinks).

Ten survivors of an Indonesian ferry, which sank with heavy loss of life, have been picked up at sea after clinging to debris for more than three days.

Here is a slightly different version of the same sentence.

Ten plucky survivors of an Indonesian ferry, which tragically sank with terrible loss of life, have been rescued at sea after bravely clinging to debris for more than three long and terrifying days.

Look at this new version. What has been added to the original? Is the original:

- more factual?
- more emotional?
- more opinion-based?
- more trustworthy?

Sentence level focus

1 News reports often use many complex sentences. For example:

Ten survivors of an Indonesian ferry, which sank with heavy loss of life, have been picked up at sea after clinging to debris for more than three days.

Look at it now in simple sentences:

There were ten survivors of an Indonesian ferry. It sank. Many people died. The survivors have been picked up. They were clinging to debris. They were in the sea for more than three days.

Why has this report been written in complex sentences? Why would the second version in simple sentences not work?

Science report

You probably have to write scientific reports after an experiment in a science lesson. These describe how the experiment worked, saying what you did, giving the results, and then drawing conclusions from the results. These are very factual reports, with no personal aspect.

Which paper towel is the strongest?

Aim

Our investigation was designed to find out which paper tissues are the strongest when wet. We tested this by setting up the equipment with a clamp and a bulldog clip fastened to the top. We then clipped a tissue to it and added another clip at the bottom with a mass weight on it. This would tell us which paper tissue was the strongest when wet.

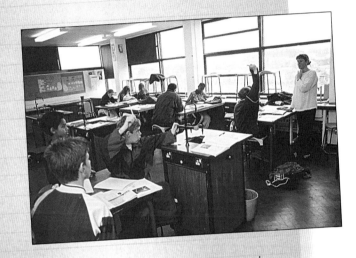

Method

We used three different types of paper tissue: laboratory towel, Fiesta quilted towel and Winfield quilted towel. We started by wetting the tissue and then attaching each one to the clips. We then added masses one by one until the tissue ripped. We repeated this three times for each paper tissue. We wrote down the results of how much mass each paper tissue could hold and then worked out the average.

Results

Type of paper tissue	Mass needed to rip the paper (g)			
	1	2	3	Average
Laboratory towel	900	800	800	833
Fiesta quilted	700	500	500	566
Winfield towel	800	700	700	733

Conclusion

Our investigation showed that the laboratory towel was the strongest paper even though it was not quilted because it had the highest mass average. This means that it would be the strongest to use and might last a little longer than the others. We discovered that the other towels were less effective and did not work as well.

Facts, facts, facts

Text level focus

1 What features are included to provide information for the reader?

2 The text begins with a question – 'Which paper towel is the strongest?' Why do you think the writer begins with this?

3 This sort of report has four headings:

- Aim
- Method
- Results
- Conclusion

Write a sentence summarizing what each one is about (what is the purpose of each section?). Try to explain why this text type needs to be written in this order.

4 What is the relationship between the question at the beginning and the 'Conclusion' paragraph?

5 The 'Method' paragraph says how the experiment was done. What order does it tell the actions in? Write down three phrases that show you this order.

6 How would you describe the style of the writing, and why?

- informative
- factual
- personal
- persuasive

Sentence level focus

1 The writer uses the past tense. Why?

2 Most of the sentences are simple or compound. Why do you think the writer chose to use these sentence types?

Word level focus

1 Look at these words from the report. Each one has a scientific meaning here, but also a more general one that is used every day. Match up each word with its scientific and general meanings.

Word from the report	Scientific meaning	General meaning
investigation	weight	normal
mass	description of what is done	a lot of
average	experiment	way
method	number got by adding the results together and dividing by the number of results	finding out about something

Writing a report

You are a TV journalist and receive an e-mail about a breaking story. You have to devise the report for the lunchtime news. Here is the e-mail.

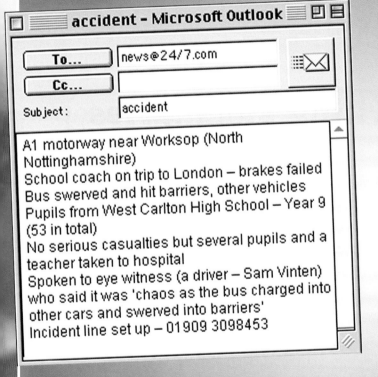

accident - Microsoft Outlook

To... news@24/7.com

Cc...

Subject: accident

A1 motorway near Worksop (North Nottinghamshire)
School coach on trip to London – brakes failed
Bus swerved and hit barriers, other vehicles
Pupils from West Carlton High School – Year 9 (53 in total)
No serious casualties but several pupils and a teacher taken to hospital
Spoken to eye witness (a driver – Sam Vinten) who said it was 'chaos as the bus charged into other cars and swerved into barriers'
Incident line set up – 01909 3098453

Research and planning

- Use the e-mail as the basis for the story – you can add a few extra details but make sure that they fit in with the story you have already.
- Decide the running order of the story.
- Make sure you include details of the school and the year group, so that only parents of those pupils will ring the incident line.

Advice on structure and language

- Use the past tense.
- Use temporal markers to sequence the text clearly (in chronological order).
- Keep it factual (unless you use eye-witness accounts that are opinion-based).
- Remember to focus on telling what happened.
- Use complex sentences to build up detail.
- If you decide to make the report two parts – the newsreader in the studio and the on-the-spot reporter – make sure the newsreader just gives a general summary and the reporter expands on the information given.

Drafting

- Check that you are not saying too much – keep the pace and flow going.
- Don't be afraid of editing or moving bits to other points.
- Check that your style is formal and factual.

Revising

- Imagine that you are reading it on the news! Is it concise and to the point? Are there any parts that are irrelevant and could be cut?

Summing up

 Exploring summaries

In pairs, take turns to tell one another what you did last weekend. Allow two minutes each, to describe what you did in some detail. Immediately after your partner has told you, write down what they said in just two sentences.

What decisions did you have to make when writing it down?

- Did you cut bits out?

- Did you focus on key points or the most interesting things?

You have just summarized what your partner said.

The key to writing summaries

Summaries are shorter versions of a longer text. To write a summary:

- focus on some key points and leave out other information

- you can present the information differently from a longer text

- you can write in full sentences or incomplete ones.

Now look at these two extracts. One is the main piece, the other a summary. As you read them, think about how they are different.

A Biography of Elizabeth I from DVD booklet

ELIZABETH

On September 7th, 1533 at the Royal Palace of Greenwich, a princess was born. To her father she was another disappointment; to her mother she was a step nearer the gallows; to her people she would become Gloriana – Queen Elizabeth I of England.

Elizabeth was born into an uncertain and dangerous world. Her father King Henry VIII was a turbulent, violent but magnificent character. After his first wife, Catherine of Aragon, bore him only a daughter – later

Queen Mary – he had quickly petitioned the Pope for a divorce so he might marry his new favourite, the beautiful Anne Boleyn. The Pope had refused but Henry was not a man to be crossed. To win Anne for himself, he dismantled a thousand years of Catholicism in England with a single stroke, making himself head of the new Protestant Church of England and granting himself a divorce. The Pope, perhaps the most powerful man on earth, was to have no say in the running of England. All Europe held its breath.

Then on that September day in 1533 Anne Boleyn rewarded Henry's dedication with the birth of a girl, Elizabeth. In a time when a male heir was considered the only true source of stability, Henry was bitterly disappointed and Anne's position became fatally undermined. Before Elizabeth had reached her third birthday her mother had been sent to the Tower of London on patently invented charges of adultery and treason and beheaded. Henry had his marriage to Anne declared invalid and Elizabeth illegitimate. She was moved away from court in London to Hatfield House, a lonely and sombre little girl. Within days Henry married his third wife, Jane Seymour, who bore the King a son. Elizabeth grew less important by the day.

B Summary biography of Elizabeth I

Elizabeth I

- Elizabeth was born on 7/9/1533, in Greenwich, London.
- She was the daughter of Henry VIII and Anne Boleyn.
- Her father had broken from the Catholic Church and created the Church of England after divorcing his first wife and marrying Anne Boleyn.
- Before Elizabeth was three years old, her mother was imprisoned in the Tower of London on charges of treason and adultery.
- Anne Boleyn was beheaded and Elizabeth was declared illegitimate.
- Elizabeth was sent away from court.
- Henry VIII married Jane Seymour and his male heir was delivered shortly after.

Text level focus

1 Summaries often simplify the language and style of the original. What obvious differences can you notice between the two pieces?

2 Which one is for a more able reader? How can you tell?

3 Compare how the two texts have been presented. Which one is easier to use?

4 Summaries usually have to leave out some information from the original text.

a What information has been removed in text B?

b Why do you think these points were cut?

5 Which version of the text do you prefer and why?

Sentence level focus

1 In the full version the writer uses complex sentences but this is not really the case in the summary. Why?

2 The writer has made the summary easy to follow by using mainly simple and compound sentences.

Look at these examples of complex sentences from the first version of the text. Rework them into simple and compound sentences. Don't be afraid to edit parts out if you think they are not really important.

a To win Anne for himself, he dismantled a thousand years of Catholicism in England with a single stroke, making himself head of the new Protestant Church of England and granting himself a divorce.

b In a time when a male heir was considered the only true source of stability, Henry was bitterly disappointed and Anne's position became fatally undermined.

> A simple sentence contains one idea, e.g.
> Elizabeth was sent away from court.
>
> A compound sentence contains two or more clauses linked by 'and', 'or', or 'but', e.g.
> Anne Boleyn was beheaded and Elizabeth was sent away.
>
> A complex sentence is made up of a main clause, which would make sense on its own – and one or more subordinate clauses, which add more information, but would not make sense on their own:
> Before Elizabeth was three, her mother was imprisoned.
>
> subordinate clause   main clause
> (would not work on its own)   (works on its own)

Word level focus

1 Some of the vocabulary in the first text is rather difficult – words such as:

   turbulent   dismantled

   dedication   petitioned

   patently   sombre

   undermined

If these words had been kept in the summary, can you suggest alternative but simpler words or phrases to use?

Writing a summary

You are going to write a summary of 80–90 words, based on the text below. Your summary will feature as part of an actor profile in a booklet to accompany the film on DVD.

Read this extract from a biography on the actor Ewan McGregor. This part centres on his role in the film *Star Wars – The Phantom Menace*.

Star Wars was unlike anything McGregor had ever experienced before. It was the biggest film he had worked on, but also the most restrictive. With directors like Danny Boyle, he was able to make suggestions and improvise. Often, he was encouraged to do so. But with Lucas the actors were only a tiny part of the equation. In the great scheme of things the actual shoot was minute in comparison to the planned 18 months of post-production, when the all-important special effects would be added. Only two of the 50 sets at Leavesden were complete – the rest would have their virtual backgrounds and effects inserted back in Los Angeles. As a result, McGregor did much of his work against 'bluescreen', the blank canvas upon which the special effects wizards would work their magic.

Although the actor found this tightly structured approach utterly frustrating, he understood the need for it. And despite the fact that the shoot was incredibly hard work, he loved it – even though the script did little to stretch his acting talents. He joked about the limits of the dialogue, recalling how there was a lot of fighting and frowning – and not much else. How many different kinds of frown could he adopt for the camera, he wondered.

Research and planning

- Decide which parts are worth keeping and will interest the reader most.
- Copy out the parts that you want to keep as a basis for your summary writing.

Advice on structure and language

- Reduce the original text, in your own words.
- Simplify difficult words and cut out unimportant ones.
- Change sentence lengths e.g.
  It was, eventually, in 1986 that Tom Cruise had his biggest break in the action romance film Top Gun
  might change to
  Tom Cruise's break came in 1986 in Top Gun.
- You can use bullet points instead of paragraphs to divide up your writing.

Drafting

- Check that you keep the main ideas of the original.
- Stick to the word limit – keep reducing your sentences down.

Revising

- Ask a friend to read it – does it tell them the key ideas? Is it too long?

In your own words

Do you keep a diary? If so, what do you write in it?

You probably write about important events, things people did and said, and how you felt about them.

Diaries are just one form of personal writing – they focus on the writer and their feelings. Autobiographies are similar – the writer tells their life story. But rather than saying what happened every day, they just pick out the important events. The focus is still on them, though – their character, and their feelings about what happened.

Exploring personal writing

Here are two extracts from very different kinds of autobiographies.

A

From
An Evil Cradling
by Brian Keenan

I sat still, then I stood up again, feeling along the edges of the bed to confirm what it was. I stood in silence trying to listen. Was there another person in the room? It was a habit with the guards to stand in silence behind you and wait until you tried to remove your blindfold, which would give them justification for beating or abuse. I stood desperately straining to hear if there was anyone else there. How long I stood I can't remember. Then telling myself that they had left, I slowly raised my hand to my face and very slowly, very cautiously lifted the end of the blindfold from my eye while lifting my head so that I could look from under it without removing it. Nothing happened, no one struck me and as I peered out from beneath the blindfold I could see two feet. Raising my head slowly, I followed the line of the feet along the legs. Whoever was in this room with me was sitting on the floor. It could not possibly be a guard.

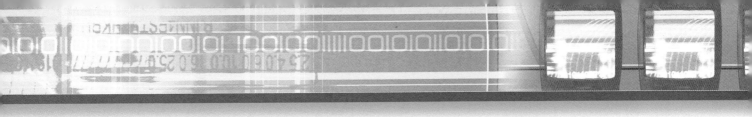

From
DAVID BECKHAM
MY STORY

Once all the waiting was over and the competition started, I was bursting with anticipation to go out and prove myself on the biggest football stage there is. I did not take it for granted that I would be picked. No professional should ever do that. But I reckoned I had done enough in the qualifying campaign to have earned my place. You could imagine my feelings, when a couple of days before our first match against Tunisia, Glenn Hoddle called the squad together, announced his team – and I was not in it. I had been given no inkling beforehand that the axe was about to fall.

I felt numb at first. I just could not get my head round the fact that I would not be kicking off the World Cup in England's starting line-up. I would not normally question a manager's or coach's decision but I felt I owed it to myself to seek an explanation from Glenn Hoddle. So I requested a meeting with him on his own and asked him direct: 'Why have I been left out?'

His answer confused me at first – then it merely added to the pain and frustration I had been feeling since he announced the team. Glenn said he did not think I was focussed enough for such a big game. I did not understand what he meant and he seemed reluctant to go into greater detail.

Start by looking at what these texts – both examples of personal recounts – have in common. The questions below should help you see the similarities.

a What are both writers trying to do?

b Do you learn anything about what the authors are like, from what they have written?

c Can you find phrases in the texts that tell you what each writer was feeling?

d What tense do the writers use?

e Pick out the temporal connectives the writers have used (markers explaining time changes, like 'a few days before', 'after five minutes', 'later'). How do these help to show the sequence of events?

Now see how the texts differ.

f Does one text give you a better idea of the atmosphere of the situation it describes?

g Do you get a better idea of what one writer is like than the other?

h Does one writer refer to his senses (sight, hearing, touch, smell, taste) more than the other?

i Now look at this section of the David Beckham text which has been re-written in an impersonal style. Compare it to the original. Which version gives a stronger impression of how David Beckham felt at the time? Which one contains more comments describing his thoughts? Which one feels more personal?

> Once all the waiting was over and the competition started, Beckham was keen to prove himself on the field. He did not take it for granted that he would be picked but he thought that he had done enough in the qualifying campaign to have earned his place. When a couple of days before the first match against Tunisia, Glenn Hoddle called the squad together and Beckham was not part of the team, he was shattered.

 # The key to writing personal recounts

When you are writing a personal recount, you should:

- write in the first person singular ('I')
- write in the past tense
- describe events from your life, usually in the order they happened (chronological order)
- express how you felt about the events at the time

- give a strong impression of your character and/or the atmosphere of the situations described
- use temporal connectives to show the order things happened in
- refer to your senses to add to the atmosphere.

A Time of Terror by James Cameron

James Cameron is known for his documentary writing and personal accounts of racial violence in 1930s USA. This extract comes from his book subtitled A Survivor's Story. In it he documents the events which overtook him when he was sixteen – ending up with him and a friend being dragged out of jail to be hanged simply because they were black.

The Crooked Path

I could hear the springs of my mother's sofa bed creaking as she got up to answer the knocking. I jumped out of bed and moved quietly and quickly to a dingy porthole window on the side of the house, and looked out into the streets below. Marie and Della were still asleep.

Cars, trucks, and policemen in blue uniforms – more than I had ever seen at one time – surrounded our house, and they were approaching with drawn revolvers. First one spotlight, then two, and, finally, a dozen or more it seemed, began raking the house from every angle. I crouched below the window, cringing, wishing again that I could disappear and start my life over again.

'Who is it?' I heard my mother ask.

'The police,' a gruff voice answered. 'Open up!'

I summoned what little courage I had left to sneak to the top of the stairs just as my mother opened the door. Light coming from the searchlights outside the house flooded the bottom of the steps. 'What do you want?' Mother asked them, nervously.

'Does James Cameron live here?' the officer wanted to know. It was the same gruff voice that answered with a demand. His question sounded more like an accusation.

'Yes,' my mother told him. And then, sensing real trouble, she broke into uncontrollable tears that sounded almost hysterical. Words began tumbling out of her mouth, rushing between sobs. 'What's he done? What do you want him for? He's a good boy. He's my only son. There must be some mistake…!'

The police cut her off. 'Where is he?'

Mother told them I was upstairs asleep in bed. Then she begged them again to tell her why I was wanted.

'Oh, Lord, have mercy!' I heard my mother cry out. 'Give me strength, dear Jesus. Help me!' Her voice trailed off and her words were lost in a fresh torrent of tears.

Without another word, the policemen began moving toward the stairway, their steps as heavy and foreboding as an army of giants invading our world from another planet. I slipped back into the bed – I don't know why – and pretended I was asleep. The heavy footsteps grew louder and louder and louder. Even with my eyelids closed in simulated sleep, I could feel the powerful beams of the officers' flashlights playing all over my body.

'That's him!' I heard someone say, as rough hands reached out and shook me. I opened my eyes wide. The room was jammed with policemen. Every one of them seemed to be ten feet tall and five feet wide. They moved about like the shadowy nameless creatures I had seen in some of my nightmares. For what seemed like a long time, no one spoke. Finally, a voice that I recognized said, 'Get up out of that bed and put your clothes on!' There was no mistaking that demand.

Text level focus

1 This kind of text tends to be written in chronological order (going in sequence from start to finish). Does the writer use chronological order here?

2 In this extract, James Cameron sometimes uses very short paragraphs for dramatic effect. Find an example of this.

3 Personal writing often refers to the writer's senses.

a Find a reference to James Cameron's:
  • sense of hearing
  • sense of sight
  • sense of touch.

b How do these references to his senses build up the atmosphere and tension?

4 The writer uses quite a lot of dialogue in the extract. For example:

'Oh, Lord, have mercy! … Give me strength, dear Jesus. Help me!'

a Why does the writer include dialogue? Select from these answers:

- to keep the plot moving and to build up tension
- to make the extract longer
- to reveal a character's thoughts and feelings.

b How different do you think this extract would be without dialogue? Take a short section and read it, missing out the dialogue. What happens?

5 Personal writing aims to give a strong impression of the author's character and/or the situation described. Which do you get a stronger impression of from this extract, and why?

Sentence level focus

1 Autobiographical writing is usually written in the first person singular ('I'). Find an example of this in the text.

2 Which tense does the writer use here? Why do you think he uses it?

3 Personal recounts usually use discourse markers to show the passing of time. Which phrases in this sentence are used to do this?

First one spotlight, then two, and, finally, a dozen or more it seemed, began raking the house from every angle.

4 The writer uses phrases like 'I crouched beneath the window, cringing' to show how he was feeling. Can you find two more phrases where he expresses his emotions like this?

5 The writer uses imagery to help the reader build a picture of the scene. Look at these examples. For each one explain what effect you think these images have.

Image	Effect
First one spotlight, then two, and, finally, a dozen or more it seemed, began raking the house from every angle.	'raking' suggests the lights searching him out carefully, leaving no stone unturned
Their steps as heavy and foreboding as an army of giants invading our world from another planet.	
They moved about like the shadowy nameless creatures I had seen in some of my nightmares.	

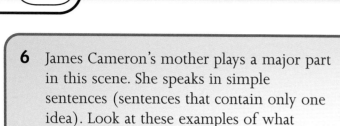

6 James Cameron's mother plays a major part in this scene. She speaks in simple sentences (sentences that contain only one idea). Look at these examples of what she says:

a 'Yes,' my mother told him.
'What's he done?'

b 'What do you want him for?'

c 'He's a good boy.'

d 'He's my only son'

e 'There must be some mistake…!'

f 'Oh, Lord have mercy!'

g 'Give me strength, dear Jesus. Help me!'

Copy out and complete the chart below to sort the examples out into statements, questions and exclamations.

Statements	Questions	Exclamations

7 What impression do you get of the mother's feelings from the way she talks in such short sentences?

Word level focus

1 Personal recounts can use powerful vocabulary to build up strong impressions.

a Look at these examples and put the highlighted words into the correct category: verbs (action words), adjectives (descriptive words) and adverbs (words that describe a verb, e.g. how something is done).

Verbs	Adjectives	Adverbs

- a dingy porthole window
- I crouched below the window
- She broke into uncontrollable tears
- Words began tumbling out of her mouth
- The heavy footsteps grew louder
- I jumped out of bed
- The room was jammed with policemen
- I opened my eyes wide

> Verb: an action word, e.g. I *go*, he *was jumping*
>
> Adjective: a word that describes a noun, e.g. the room was *dark*, a *cold* night
>
> Adverb: a word that describes a verb, e.g. I go *slowly*, he was jumping *high*

b Now look at these examples. The first one is the original and the second is an altered version. Which version works best for each one? Why?

- Words began tumbling out of her mouth
- Words began coming out of her mouth

- I jumped out of bed
- I got out of bed

- The room was jammed with policemen
- The room was full of policemen

Writing a personal recount

You are going to construct your own text based on what you have learned in this unit.

Think about an event in your life that has had an effect or impact on you; one you know you will never forget. It might be when something new or different happened, for example:

- a visit
- a memorable birthday
- the first flight you experienced
- a trip to somewhere really exotic or different
- getting a new pet
- what you did at the Millennium
- an accident or crisis.

Research and planning

- Decide on the event.

- Remember, this is a very personal form of writing, so you can include details about yourself and how you felt.

- Get together the key points that you want to make – you can cut the boring bits and focus on the interesting and lively parts (nobody will know except you!).

Advice on structure and language

- Decide on a logical running order – but remember these texts are usually written in chronological order (the order things happened in).

- Use temporal connectives to indicate time and place.

- Use the first person singular 'I' or plural 'we'.

- Write in the past tense as the events have already happened.

- Use different sentence types to control the text. (Compound and complex sentences help to build up the detail and create a more sophisticated feel; simple sentences can be used for dramatic effect or to stress the importance of a point.)

- Use lively and interesting language – help the reader to picture the scene by referring to all your senses or using imagery.

- Be **personal** and remember to give the reader some idea of what you are like; be honest in what you say.

Drafting

- Check that you are keeping it lively and well paced.

- Check that you are varying your use of language to keep the reader alert.

- Make sure that the reader gets a real sense of what happened.

Revising

- Cut any bits that seem dull or go off the subject – get a partner to check and give their opinion.

- Is it personal? Does the reader get some sense of how you felt?

Changing minds

While many non-fiction texts exist mainly to inform or advise, a range of texts have persuasion as their purpose. They may work in different ways, depending on the kind of text. In this unit, you will explore three different kinds of persuasive texts. These are campaigning texts, which are obviously persuasive; reviews, which exist to inform and persuade; and editorials and speeches, which are based on the assumption that the reader or listener feels the same about the subject as the speaker or writer.

Exploring campaigning texts

There are many different types of persuasive texts such as adverts on television and radio, in magazines and newspapers, leaflets, fliers, and campaign letters. These texts all aim to persuade you to adopt a certain point of view – they try to convince you that they are right. They use specific techniques to do this. Try this activity to find out more.

Divide into small groups and each take a task below.

1 How would you persuade people to give up smoking? List your ideas.	**2** Think of an image for a poster on alcohol abuse that would have an impact.	**3** Devise a slogan (no more than 10 words) for a poster to stop people from speeding.	**4** Write the opening paragraph for a leaflet persuading people to give money to a charity for the homeless.

Now you're going to look at your ideas.

• Which ones are the best? (Which ones catch your attention? Which ones make you want to take action?)

• What makes them good? How do they make their impact?

Through particularly powerful words?

Words like 'shocking', 'deadly', 'hopeless', 'vulnerable' – these are all meant to have an impact on the reader's feelings (they are also called emotive words).

Through shocking images?

Pictures can have much more impact than words – they stay in someone's mind much longer. Also it is much harder to argue with a picture.

By focusing on individual stories?

'Home for Jim was on a windswept hill amongst some brambles. His dearest wish was to make a fresh start.' – discussing specific people is a way of making the situation 'real' for the reader, and making them want to help.

Through statistics?

'Over 600 people a year die on the roads.' – statistics add weight to an argument.

By predicting the worst?

'Smoking can lead to poor general health, amputations and death by lung cancer.' – predicting the worst can be very persuasive. The dramatic situation predicted arouses the reader's fear or sympathy, and makes them want to stop it happening.

By subtly introducing opinions?

'Teenage tearaway Ben in evil break-in plot' – the highlighted words show the writer's opinion, but are slotted in to make it look like fact.

The key to writing campaigning texts

To write an effective campaign text, you could:

- use emotive words and phrases, to appeal to your reader's feelings
- show images that may be shocking or designed to arouse the reader's sympathy
- focus on individual stories
- use statistics to give weight to your argument
- introduce opinions subtly to sway the reader.

WWF leaflet

WWF-UK, Panda House,
Weyside Park, Catteshall Lane,
Godalming, Surrey GU7 1XR
Website: http://www.wwf-uk.org

Telephone: 01483 426444
Fax: 01483 426409

By the end of the century, black rhinos could be gone from the earth forever.

Dear Friend,

The statistics are truly horrific. During the seventies, Kenya lost 90% of its black rhino population; they were brutally slaughtered by illegal poachers. Their numbers plummeted from 20,000 in 1970 to just 350 in 1983.

The rhinos were slaughtered for their precious horns. Sometimes it was because people in the Far East believed the rhino horn had medicinal value. Sometimes it was to use the horns for handles on ornamental daggers. But always, the result was just the same.

Then in 1992, WWF began funding the Kenya Wildlife Service Black Rhino project, involving an extensive protection and management programme. Twelve sanctuaries throughout the country were established and together they have succeeded in raising the total black rhino population to its current number of 462.

But while rhino horn can still fetch three times its weight in gold on the black market, these creatures remain a vulnerable target to poachers. We are doing everything we can to prevent this illegal trade and wipe out the demand for rhino horn once and for all.

Kinyanjui

Little Naomi

In the meantime, we must continue to provide protection for those magnificent creatures that still survive. But to do so, we desperately need your help.

We must, for example, keep the Kenyan black rhino protection project going for another year. Which means that we must find the money now to purchase vital equipment such as VHF radios, tracking equipment, binoculars, and various other supplies for rhino monitoring and surveillance.

Time is running out. The population of black rhinos in Kenya sits precariously at 462. Without your help now, we will not be able to continue protecting these creatures, and by the end of the century they could be gone from our planet forever. We won't have another chance to save them.

You can help us by adopting a rhino.

By adopting a rhino, your support not only funds the Kenyan black rhino project, but helps fund WWF's rhino conservation work throughout Africa and Asia.

One of the Kenya Wildlife Service guards protecting the black rhinos.

Your generosity will entitle you to a Certificate of Adoption, a photo and details of your rhino. Also, we promise to keep you informed of your rhino's progress by sending you regular updates of their well-being.

Please help us today by completing the enclosed Adoption Application. It could be our final chance to help save rhinos from disappearing forever.

Yours sincerely,

Lilian and her family, Ejore and Emma

Richard Barnwell
Head of Africa Programme, WWF-UK

President: HRH Princess Alexandra, the Hon. Lady Ogilvy GCVO, Chairman: Sara Morrison, Chief Executive: Robert Napier
Registered Charity number 201707. VAT number 244 2516 81. September 1998

75

Text level focus

1 Look at how this text opens. It begins with a statement that is then developed with facts, figures and opinions:

The statistics are truly horrific. During the seventies, Kenya lost 90% of its black rhino population; they were brutally slaughtered by illegal poachers. Their numbers plummeted from 20,000 in 1970 to just 350 in 1983.

a What is fact here and what is opinion?

b How effective do you find this as an opening to the text?

2 Campaigning texts often try to make the situation they are describing seem urgent. How does the WWF do this in paragraph 7?

3 How are statistics used in paragraph 1 to show what the situation is like?

4 How is this text set out to make the reader want to read it?

5 Why do you think the writer names the rhinos in the pictures? How is this meant to persuade you to give money?

6 The writer structures the text by frequently mentioning dates and time. Look at how this is done by focusing on:

- the end of paragraph 1
- the beginnings of paragraphs 3, 5, 7 and 11.

What do you notice about the sequence of the argument? (Look at how the time changes from the first date to the last paragraph.)

7 Look at the final paragraph and compare it with the first one. How does this link the whole text together and conclude the leaflet?

8 Predicting the worst is another feature of campaigning texts. Can you find an example of this? Why do you think the writer does this?

9 On a scale of 1 to 10 (1 as the lowest and 10 the highest), how persuasive do you find this text? Explain your reasons with examples.

Sentence level focus

1 Simple sentences convey one main idea. These are used at several points in the letter, for example:

- But *always*, the result was just the same. *(paragraph 2)*

- Time is running out. *(paragraph 7)*

a What effect do these sentence types have?

b Would longer, more complex sentences work as well in these places? Look at this adapted version of paragraph 7:

Time is running out as the population of black rhinos in Kenya sits precariously at 462.

How does it change the writer's effect?

2 Find paragraph 8. Why is this sentence in its own paragraph?

3 In most persuasive texts the writer uses the present tense to show how the problem is happening now. However, in this leaflet the writer uses the past, present and future. Find an example of each tense being used and then explain why the writer uses all three tenses.

4 In paragraph 9 the writer says:

By adopting a rhino, your support not only funds the Kenyan black rhino project, but helps fund WWF's rhino conservation work throughout Africa and Asia.

What is the effect of saying 'not only… but…'?

5 One way of persuading people is to use modal verbs. These include 'should', 'could', 'would', 'must', 'ought to', 'may', 'might', 'need to'.

In paragraphs 5 and 6 the writer uses 'must' a few times. Try reading these examples from the paragraphs, replacing 'must' with other modal verbs:

- We must continue to provide protection for those magnificent creatures that still survive.

- We must, for example, keep the Kenyan black rhino protection project going for another year.

What happens to the impact of the message? Which modals work best and which are not so good?

Word level focus

1 Campaigning texts often use powerful language to affect the reader's emotions. Look at these words from the leaflet. Which ones you say were deliberately used for effect?

horrific	brutally	slaughtered
vulnerable	wipe out	protection
desperately	creatures	forever
century		

Writing a campaigning text

Design a leaflet to persuade people to give money to a charity for the homeless.

Research and planning

- Decide on key points – such as what life is like for a homeless person (perhaps focus on one person), why the charity needs money, how the charity will spend it.

- Think of a suitable name for your charity – something easy to remember.

- Only use important points – keep it snappy and direct.

Advice on structure and language

- Think about how to present your leaflet.

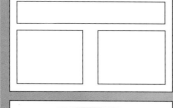

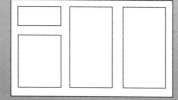

- Use the present tense.

- Use a range of sentence types for effect: simple sentences for emphasis, and longer, more complex sentences to build up detail.

- Use statistics to shock, or to back up your argument.

- Use powerful language to affect your readers' emotions and subtly introduce opinions.

- Think about using powerful pictures to illustrate your leaflet.

- Build up emphasis through repetition.

Drafting

- Begin taking your ideas and applying the above features to make it sound really persuasive.

- Check with other students and read each other's work.

Revising

- Does your text feel persuasive? Compare it with the WWF leaflet. What can you improve?

Exploring reviews

Do you ever talk with friends about films you've seen? About books you've read or games you've played on a PC or console? If you do then you'll probably be saying what you think about them; whether they are good or bad. You are giving a review of them.

Here are two short film reviews. Read them, and think about these questions with a partner.

1 Reviews are usually written with this sort of structure:

- opening statement
- plot summary
- reviewer's opinion

Does this structure work here?

2 When the reviewer says what they think, they are giving their opinion and personal response to the film, book, or game. Pick out words in both examples that clearly show the writers' opinions.

3 Noun phrases are phrases made from a noun and one or more adjectives (describing words) – like 'a fun-packed gross-out comedy'. Writers often use them to fit a lot of information into a small space. Can you find any noun phrases in these reviews?

Romeo Must Die (15)☆☆☆

Martial artist Jet Li headlines this action-packed kung fu movie loosely based on Romeo and Juliet. He plays an ex Hong Kong cop who busts out of prison and heads straight for San Francisco to avenge the gangland murder of his brother. It's not the most believable of plots, but the fight scenes are breathtaking. Singer Aaliyah makes a lively love interest and trills out 4 of the soundtrack songs – reason alone to see this film in our book.

Billy Elliot (15)

It might be a small story – young lad Billy fights for his right to be a ballet dancer – but this emotional rollercoaster ride will reduce you to a quivering wreck and fill your heart with joy. A deserved box-office triumph.

You may have picked out these features:

- Both reviews start with an opening statement – review A's is 'Martial artist Jet Li headlines this action-packed kung fu movie loosely based on Romeo and Juliet'.

- Both reviews feature a plot summary – review B's is 'young lad Billy fights for his right to be a ballet dancer'.

- Both texts end with the reviewer's overall opinion of the film – review B says 'this emotional rollercoaster ride will reduce you to a quivering wreck and fill your heart with joy. A deserved box-office triumph'.

- Both reviewers give their opinions throughout, in words like 'action-packed' and 'breathtaking'.

- Both reviews also use noun phrases to pack the information into a short review: 'young lad Billy', and 'emotional rollercoaster ride' are two from review B.

 # The key to writing reviews

When you are writing a review, write in the present tense and include:

- an opening statement about what is being reviewed

- a summary of the plot (if it's a book or film) or an overview of the music or events (if it's a CD or game)

- your opinion (include language that is clearly opinion-based and personal, as well as emotive language to sway your reader's response)

- noun phrases to put across information and opinions easily.

Film review

We come across reviews all over the place: in magazines, in newspapers, on television and when we discuss our own ideas and opinions on things such as music, films, books, clothes, football matches and so on.

This review is from a school website.

Tarzan

Review by Lisa Freinkman

The story of Tarzan is hardly a new one. What's new about this animated Disney remake is the eye-popping 3D graphics – and, of course, the soundtrack by *N SYNC and Phil Collins (yeah, I hadn't heard of him, either).

The storytelling here is standard Disney fare. Baby Tarzan and his parents survive a shipwreck and make their home on a jungle island. Then Mr. and Mrs. Tarzan are killed by a leopard, and the bouncing baby boy is 'adopted' by a lovable gorilla who has just lost her baby. As Tarzan grows up, he must deal with being different – and distrusted by Kerchak, apparently the only adult male in the group of gorillas (just one of the many things in this movie that are not exactly appropriate for Disney's target audience of young children). Eventually, Jane and her father appear in the jungle to study gorillas, aided by an enormous, decidedly evil-looking man with a gun. Jane meets Tarzan when he saves her from a pack of angry baboons, in one of the best sequences of the film. She teaches him about the civilized world through a series of slides that she just happens to have brought along on her jungle adventure, and the movie builds towards the inevitable action climax and happy conclusion.

Once again, the graphics are great, and the soundtrack wasn't too grating even for this anti-*N SYNC activist. The animation aims to make the viewer feel as if he or she is leaping from vine to vine along with Tarzan, and this is often accomplished through camera tricks similar to the ones in the famous Gap commercials. However, don't necessarily rent this for your little brother or sister. The fight scenes are violent and will probably frighten them, and the deaths of Kerchak and the evil human character are also more than a little dark. Little kids will also be confused by the fact that we always hear the gorillas and Tarzan speaking English, until Tarzan brings Jane along and starts talking in the 'oo-oo-ee' dialect of the apes. So, to recap, 'Tarzan' is fun to watch, but nothing out of the ordinary for Disney.

Text level focus

1 Reviews tend to serve purposes such as informing the reader, recommending or criticizing something. What do you think the purposes are of this review?

2 A review works through a mixture of fact (what is true) and opinion (what the reviewer thinks).

   a Skim through the review once more and write down two facts and two opinions. Highlight the words which show you the opinions.
   For example:

   So, to recap, Tarzan is fun to watch, but nothing out of the ordinary for Disney.

   - Fact – Tarzan is the name of the film and it's by Disney.

   - Opinion – it's 'fun to watch' but 'nothing out of the ordinary' (this is what the reviewer thinks).

   b Now decide – is the review more factual or opinion based?

3 Reviews often begin with fact-based information before moving on to the writer's opinions. Is this true of this review or does the writer offer her opinions from the start?

4 What does the reviewer think of this film? Does she like it or does she think it could be better? Look at this list of extracts from the review and decide whether they are positive or negative about the film. Copy out the grid below and use it to sort the points out.

   a What's new about this animated Disney remake is the eye-popping 3D graphics…

   b … just one of the many things in this movie that are not exactly appropriate for Disney's target audience of young children…

   c Jane meets Tarzan when he saves her from a pack of angry baboons, in one of the best sequences of the film.

   d Once again, the graphics are great, and the soundtrack wasn't too grating…

   e Don't necessarily rent this for your little brother or sister. The fight scenes are violent and will probably frighten them…

   f Little kids will also be confused by the fact that we always hear the gorillas and Tarzan speaking English…

   g So to recap, Tarzan is fun to watch, but nothing out of the ordinary…

   Look at your results. Do you think the writer is more positive or negative about the film?

Does she like it?	Could it be better?

Sentence level focus

1 One way writers add detail to reviews is by using noun phrases. These are typical examples from this review:

- Eye-popping 3D graphics
- Bouncing baby boy
- Evil-looking man

a Find two more sentences with noun phrases in them.

b Then rewrite both sentences removing them, e.g.

What's new about this animated Disney remake is the eye-popping 3D graphics…

What's new about this animated Disney remake is the graphics…

Are your new versions as persuasive as the originals?

Word level focus

1 This text contains a lot of technical words connected to films and the cinema. Write a list of these words. Why does the writer need to use specialist vocabulary here?

2 In a review the writer is telling us whether they think something is good or bad. But a good writer will use a range of synonyms to avoid repeating 'good' and 'bad', which could sound dull.

a Look back through the review and find synonyms that are used for 'good' and 'bad'. Copy and fill in the grid below.

Synonyms for good	Synonyms for bad

b Now add two more synonyms of your own to each list. You will be able to use these in the writing task later.

> Synonyms are words that mean the same as another word, or have a very similar meaning, e.g. 'wonderful' and 'fantastic' are synonyms for 'good'.

Writing a review

You are going to write a review for a teenage website on one of the following topics:

- a film or video

- a book

- a theatre performance

- a computer game.

Research and planning

- Choose a subject that you definitely have some opinions about.

- Decide on the angle that you are going to take – positive, negative, neutral.

Advice on structure and language

- Use a logical structure: firstly write an opening statement, next explain the product under review – a factual summary or overview, then give your opinion of it – what was good, what was bad.

- Use a lively and interesting style to give your opinion – use synonyms to avoid repeating words for 'good' or 'bad'.

- Try to use noun phrases to add detail and pace to your writing.

- Use emotive language to persuade your reader of your opinion.

Drafting

- Keep checking that your language is suitable for your audience.

- Try not to let it get too long. Use noun phrases to help keep it snappy.

Revising

- Does your review inform, entertain, and review the product?

Exploring speeches and editorials

Sometimes a writer might know that many people agree with their thoughts about the topic being discussed and may not aim specifically to persuade them, but to reinforce ideas they already have. For example, in September 1997 when Diana, Princess of Wales died, the newspapers all carried stories based on the assumption that everyone in Britain was sharing an experience of grief. Speeches and editorials are often based on a belief that the readers or listeners will agree with the opinions expressed.

Look at these two extracts from speeches.

A

'Hunting is our music'
by Ann Mallalieu

All of us here have given a part of our lives to be here in Hyde Park. We have come here for a reason. We cannot and will not stand by in silence and watch our countryside, our communities and our way of life destroyed for ever by misguided urban political correctness.

This rally is not just about hunting. Many perhaps most of those here today don't hunt themselves.

It is about freedom, the freedom of people to choose how they live their own lives. It is about tolerance of minorities, and sadly those who live in and work in the countryside are now a minority. It is about listening to and respecting the views of other people of which you may personally disapprove.

B

Extract from speech by Sojourner Truth, 1852

That man over there says a woman needs to be helped into carriages and lifted over ditches and to have the best place everywhere. Nobody ever helped me into carriages or over mud puddles or gives me a best place, and ain't I a woman? Look at me, look at my arm! I have ploughed and planted and gathered into barns and no man could head me, and ain't I a woman? I could work as much as and eat as much as a man – when I could get to it – and bear the lash as well, and ain't I a woman? I have borne 13 children and seen most all sold into slavery and when I cried out a mother's grief, none but Jesus heard me and ain't I a woman?

Now look at these questions. Some might refer to only one text, and others to both.

- Which pronoun is used in text A to talk to the reader/listener? Why?

- Sometimes writers of speeches and editorials set up a pattern of three ideas. Is this used in either text?

- Rhetorical questions (questions that are asked more for effect than for an answer) might be used. Can you find an example in the texts?

- Repetition (where a point or phrase is said more than once) might feature. Is this used here?

- Language can be used to appeal to the reader's/listener's emotions. Does either speaker do this?

- Occasionally simple sentences (sentences containing one idea) are used to make a point clear to the audience. Is this technique used here?

You may have spotted the following features:

- In text A the pronoun 'we' is used to address the reader/listener – to make them feel part of what is going on, and show that the speaker thinks they will agree with her.

- Both texts use patterns of three. For example, in text B: 'Nobody ever helps me into carriages, or over mud puddles, or gives me any best place'.

- Text B uses rhetorical questions – 'Ain't I a woman?' The audience listening would know that she is a woman but she is asking the question to stress the point of the inequality of black and white women.

- Text B repeats the question 'Ain't I a woman?'

- Both texts use emotive language to appeal to the audience's feelings. For example in text A: 'destroyed', 'sadly', 'minority'.

- Both examples use simple sentences for effect, such as text A's 'We have come here for a reason.'

 # The key to writing editorials and speeches

When you write an editorial or a speech, your aim is always to keep your reader or listener on your side. To do this, you can:

- use 'we' to show that you feel you have something in common with your reader or listener, and that you expect them to share the opinions expressed

- use patterns of three to build up an effect

- use repetition of key words and phrases to get them into the reader's or listener's mind

- use rhetorical questions to involve your audience

- use a range of sentences, including short simple ones for emphasis

- use emotionally-charged language to appeal to your audience's feelings.

Editorial

Nearly every newspaper contains an editorial section. This is where the editor of the newspaper reflects and discusses a topical issue or event.

This extract, from the Mirror, looks at football hooliganism during Euro 2000. England faced being thrown out of the competition due to violence from a small minority of its fans whilst in Europe.

VOICE OF The Mirror

voice@mirror.co.uk

Mere words won't stop the violence

NO Government can totally guarantee to stop all hooligans running wild at foreign soccer matches.

But it is possible to make it so tough for them that most won't bother trying to go. That's what the Germans, for instance, did very successfully in the build-up to Euro 2000.

But we've stuck our heads in the sand as usual and hoped it wouldn't be as bad as everyone said it would.

Well, it has been. In fact it's been worse.

And now we face the distinct possibility of being thrown out of the tournament because of the disgusting little yobs who've been 'flying the flag' on our behalf.

Tony Blair's furious, of course. And so's Jack Straw. And so's the FA, and so are all the other usual suspects when the hooligans rear their notably ugly heads.

But what do they actually DO about it?

Yesterday, 'Draconian' new plans were announced. Or so we were told. In fact, they were about as Draconian as a gentle tap on the tattooed wrist.

Words, words, words, words. That's always been our weapon against these drunken, violent, mindless creeps who ruin it for everyone.

It's not just a football problem. These are the same idiots who wreak havoc in every town in Britain every weekend and smash up Spain on their holidays.

Britain has the most drug-ravaged, alcoholic, criminal, abusive, and utterly obnoxious collections of young males of any European country.

And this is their big chance to show everyone just how moronic they can be.

Short of national service, there is only one way to stop them. And that is to remove all trouble-makers' passports for 10 years and bang the worst offenders in prison for at least five years.

It's too late for Euro 2000 – they are already there, and we just have to pray that some fragment of their gormless cerebral mass registers the enormity of what further fighting might do.

But Tony Blair's government must introduce severe new punishments right now to ensure that this utter disgrace cannot happen again.

Text level focus

1 The introductory paragraph is in bold. What do you think the purpose of this paragraph is?

2 Later in the text, some type is in bold or underlined in italics. Why do you think this has been done?

3 Editorial writers put their opinions across very clearly. Which of these statements best sums up this writer's opinion?

- All hooligans should pay a penalty.

- Words are not enough, the government needs tough measures to reduce violence.

- He hopes the hooligans might learn from their mistakes.

4 How would you describe the writer's tone here?

- angry
- not bothered really
- relaxed
- tired of the situation

Back up your choice with examples from the text.

5 Editorials work through a mixture of fact (something true) and opinion (something that is someone's point of view and not necessarily true). In this example, the opinions have been highlighted.

And now we face the distinct possibility of being thrown out of the tournament because of the disgusting little yobs who've been 'flying the flag' on our behalf.

Read through the editorial again, and try to pick out all the facts (take out the emotionally-charged words and this will help you). Based on what you have done, do you think the article is mainly based on facts or opinions?

Sentence level focus

1 This editorial is written in the present tense. Can you explain why?

2 Paragraph 4 reads

Well, it has been. In fact it's been worse.

Why is this in its own paragraph?

Why has the writer used two simple sentences at this point?

3 Paragraph 9 starts with repetition 'Words, words, words, words'. What effect is created here?

4 Editorials often use rhetorical questions, like this one in paragraph 9:

But what do they DO about it?

What answer is the writer hoping to generate in the readers' minds?

5 Look at the number of sentences that begin with the conjunctions (joining words) 'and' or 'but'. For example:

- *And this is their big chance to show everyone just how moronic they can be.*

- *But we've stuck our heads in the sand as usual and hoped it wouldn't be as bad as everyone said it would.*

a Find another example beginning with 'and' or 'but'.

b This is not really the accurate sort of English that your teacher would expect to see. Why do you think the writer starts sentences with 'and' or 'but'?

Word level focus

1 Editorial writers choose their words carefully to create an image in the reader's mind. What sort of image do these extracts create for you?

Extract	Image
All hooligans running wild	Creates idea of uncontrolled animal-like behaviour
The hooligans rear their notably ugly heads	
These drunken, violent, mindless creeps	

Speech

In 1982 Argentina took control of the Falkland Islands (under British rule in the South Atlantic off the coast of Argentina). The then Prime Minister, Margaret Thatcher, sent a task force of 10,000 troops to return the island to British rule. She made this speech after Britain had won the Falklands War.

The Falklands Factor

Today we meet in the aftermath of the Falklands Battle. Our country has won a great victory and we are entitled to be proud. This nation had the resolution to do what it knew had to be done – to do what it knew was right.

We fought to show that aggression does not pay, and that the robber cannot be allowed to get away with his swag. We fought with the support of so many throughout the world: the Security Council, the Commonwealth, the European Community, and the United States. Yet we also fought alone – for we fought for our own people and for our own sovereign territory.

Now that it is all over, things cannot be the same again, for we have learnt something about ourselves – a lesson which we desperately needed to learn. When we started out, there were the waverers and the faint-hearts: the people who thought that Britain could no longer seize the initiative for herself; the people who thought we could no longer do the great things which we once did; and those who believed that our decline was irreversible – that we could never again be what we were. There were those who would not admit it – even perhaps some here today – people who would have strenuously denied the suggestion but – in their heart of hearts – they too had their secret fears that it was true: that Britain was no longer the nation that had built an Empire and ruled a quarter of the world.

Well, they were wrong. The lesson of the Falklands is that Britain has not changed and that this nation still has those sterling qualities which shine through our history. This generation can match their fathers and grandfathers in ability, in courage, and in resolution. We have not changed. When the demands of war and the dangers to our own people call us to arms – then we British are as we have always been – competent, courageous and resolute.

When called to arms – ah, that's the problem. It took the battle in the South Atlantic for the shipyards to adapt ships way ahead of time; for dockyards to refit merchantmen and cruise liners, to fix helicopter platforms, to convert hospital ships –

all faster than was thought possible; it took the demands of war for every stop to be pulled out and every man and woman to do their best.

British people had to be threatened by foreign soldiers and British territory invaded and then – why then – the response was incomparable. Yet why does it need a war to bring out our qualities and reassert our pride? Why do we have to be invaded before we throw aside our selfish aims and begin to work together as only we can work, and achieve as only we can achieve?

That really is the challenge we as a nation face today. We have to see that the spirit of the South Atlantic – the real spirit of Britain – is kindled not only by war but can now be fired by peace.

We have the first prerequisite. We know we can do it – we haven't lost the ability. That is the Falklands Factor. We have proved ourselves to ourselves. It is a lesson we must not now forget. Indeed, it is a lesson which we must apply to peace just as we have learnt it in war. The faltering and the self-doubt has given way to achievement and pride. We have the confidence and we must use it.

Just look at the Task Force as an object lesson. Every man had his own task to do and did it superbly. Officers and men, senior NCO and newest recruit – every one realized that his contribution was essential for the success of the whole. All were equally valuable – each was differently qualified. By working together, each was able to do more than his best. As a team they raised the average to the level of the best and by each doing his utmost together they achieved the impossible. That's an accurate picture of Britain at war – not yet of Britain at peace. But the spirit has stirred and the nation has begun to assert itself. Things are not going to be the same again.

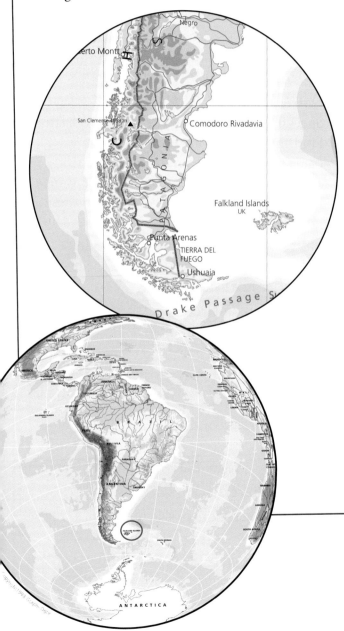

Text level focus

1 Throughout the speech Mrs Thatcher refers to the British people and Great Britain as 'we', 'our country', and 'our own people'. What effect do you think she intended this to create?

2 Speech writers should use a new paragraph for each new idea. Try to summarize the main points in one sentence each by taking the main idea from each paragraph. Does Mrs Thatcher use a new paragraph for each new idea in her speech?

3 How would you describe the style of this speech?

- patriotic and emotional
- over the top
- easy and clear

Explain what you think with a few examples to support your points.

4 Who is the audience of Mrs Thatcher's speech?
Think about:

- the pronouns she uses
- whether she seems sorry for the war
- if she tries to win people over with her speech.

Sentence level focus

1 Speeches often use patterns of three, as in this extract from paragraph 4:

This generation can match their fathers and grandfathers in ability, in courage, and in resolution. We have not changed. When the demands of war and the dangers to our own people call us to arms – then we British are as we have always been – competent, courageous and resolute.

These words in threes are all emotive.

Why do you think Mrs Thatcher uses patterns of three instead of just one word? Read both examples removing two of the highlighted words to see what happens.

2 At the end of paragraph 2 Mrs Thatcher says:

Yet we also fought alone – for we fought for our own people and for our own sovereign territory.

How does the writer use repetition here? Why do you think this is done?

3 Paragraph 3 is structured using long sentences to build up the detail:

When we started out, there were the waverers and the faint-hearts: the people who thought we could no longer do the great things which we once did; and those who believed that our decline was irreversible – that we could never again be what we were.

Paragraph 4 begins with a short, simple sentence: *Well, they were wrong.*

Why? What effect does this create?

4 Speech writers often ask rhetorical questions. Find the two rhetorical questions in paragraph 6. Then think about why Mrs Thatcher uses them – what does she want her audience to think in response to these questions?

5 Most paragraphs begin with a simple sentence, e.g. *That really is the challenge we as a nation face today.*

Explain why this is an effective way to begin and build up the argument.

Word level focus

1 In paragraph 2 pick out the metaphor (comparison) used to refer to the Argentineans by Mrs Thatcher. How has this word been used deliberately for effect?

2 Many sentences in the speech use pairs or groups of words which have opposite meanings. Look at these words, and match them up into pairs of opposites. Once you have matched them up, check back in the speech to see if you are right.

war	faltering	pride	fears
peace	best	average	courage
self-doubt	achievement		

3 Re-read this extract:

This nation had the resolution to do what it knew had o be done – to do what it knew was right.

Why is there repetition here on the words 'do' and 'done'? What does it suggest about the British?

Writing editorials and speeches

Choose one of the subjects below to write a speech or an editorial about. (Take a subject that you feel strongly about).

- School uniform (for or against)
- Smoking – is it all bad?
- Animal testing – why do we do it?
- Hunting – is it acceptable?
- Mobile phones – should they be allowed in schools?

Research and planning

- Decide on your angle in the piece – positive or negative.
- Assemble your ideas by developing five key points.
- Focus on these key points (facts and opinions) and decide on a paragraph running order.
- Remember to consider how your audience might disagree so build in your arguments against what they might think.

Advice on structure and language

- Use emotionally-charged and persuasive words and phrases – inspire your listeners to accept your point of view.
- Experiment with sentence types for effect.
- Use a pattern of three to build up your ideas.

- Use rhetorical questions to add to the style.
- Build up to a climax.
- Make your ideas link from paragraph to paragraph.
- Decide how formal or informal to make it (remember if you are too informal you might not be taken seriously and if you are too formal you may seem a bit boring).

For editorials, also remember:
Think of an eye-catching headline to grab the reader's attention.

Drafting

- Check that your style is lively and well-paced – otherwise you may lose your audience.
- Draw your audience in – use pronouns 'you', 'your', 'our', 'we'.
- Outline the topic quickly, clearly and persuasively at the beginning.

For the end of a speech, also remember:
Aim to summarize your main points, still being persuasive and positive.

Revising

- Be prepared to rework your speech or editorial and try it out on other people. Have you used all the features you can? Is your piece persuasive?

Taking sides

This unit looks at biased texts. A biased piece of writing only considers one point of view and suggests that it is the correct view.

 Exploring bias

Look at these two texts about road protests.
Both are heavily biased.

A

Highly-organized road protesters, who had dug themselves into tunnels and camped in trees to prevent the construction of the new M90 motorway, were yesterday dragged from their shelters on the site by baton-wielding police. The protesters left calmly, chanting anti-road slogans – ending in violent scuffles after the police battered down one young man. Six people were arrested as onlookers jeered at the police for this violent ending to a peaceful protest.

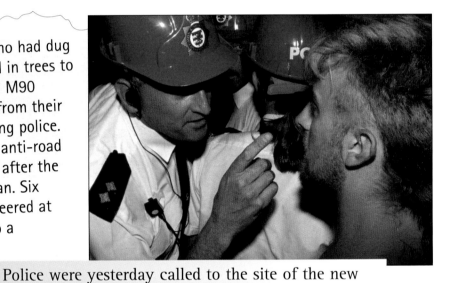

B

Police were yesterday called to the site of the new M90 motorway where a rabble of road protesters had taken to tunnelling and sitting in trees to hinder the building of this vital new road. As the police attempted to persuade the scruffy louts to leave, they chanted slogans and became violent, leaving the police no option but to use pressure. Onlookers cheered as police arrested a handful of so-called eco-warriors.

Look at both texts and answer these questions:

● Which text is biased and sides with the police?

● Which one is biased and sides with the protesters?

● How do the writers use language to make the texts biased? Do they use words which appeal to the reader's feelings (emotive language)?

● Do both texts report the same 'facts'?

You might have noticed that:

- Text B is biased in favour of the police – who are made out to be just doing their job – and against the protesters – who are presented as violent and out of control.

- Text A is biased in favour of the protesters – who are made to appear innocent but cruelly treated by the police.

- Both texts use emotive language to convince the reader. For example, in text A, the protesters are 'highly-organized' while in text B they are 'a rabble' and 'scruffy louts'.

- The texts report different 'facts', as in text A, the onlookers 'jeered at the police', while in text B, they 'cheered at the clearance of the site'.

Re-read the texts again and make a list of the real facts. What is the basic story here?

Now write a version which is not biased at all. You may need to think quite carefully, because the writer has put their opinions in quite skilfully.

 The key to writing biased texts

If you want to make a piece of writing biased, you should:

- take the view of one side
- use positive or negative language about one side (or positive about one side and negative about the other)
- use emotive language to put across your opinions
- distort the facts (or select facts) to make one side look better or worse.

When a text is biased it is harder for the reader to make their own decision about what really happened and what is best to think. Look at the next two texts. They both report the same story – but one is biased and the other is not.

The Mirror, Monday, April 3, 2000

YOKO TO MAKE £200M FROM BEATLES BOOK

But she's not written any of it

By **KEVIN O'SULLIVAN**

ALL YOU NEED IS DOUGH: Yoko, Paul, George and Ringo will coin it

YOKO Ono will pocket more than £200 million from a new Beatles book she has had absolutely nothing to do with.

The astonishing windfall for John Lennon's widow will be a quarter of the profits from the first official biography of the Fab Four.

The Beatles anthology – due out in the Autumn – has been in the pipeline for SIX YEARS, it was revealed yesterday. Sir Paul McCartney, George Harrison and Ringo Starr have had countless meetings during that time to compare notes on their 360-page book.

They, too, will make more than £200 million each.

The book, the size of an encyclopaedia, is expected to sell for around £50 and make £1 billion.

It is thought to feature up to 1,200 unpublished photos and tell the REAL story of the group's split.

A spokesman said: 'Yoko will get an equal share of the profits even though she hasn't done a thing.

'But that's the way it goes with the Beatles. Yoko always gets John's 25 per cent.

'But Paul and the boys are used to the system and they're long past begrudging Yoko the cash.'

Blamed

McCartney, 57, is understood to have persuaded Harrison, also 57, and 59-year-old Starr that it is important to put the record straight.

Some of the 400 unofficial Beatles books have blamed him for the split.

But the anthology will level that charge against Lennon.

He is said to have walked out on the group months before the nation knew.

The book will chronicle the 'warts and all' saga of the group's fame, drug-taking and womanizing.

It will reveal their jealousies and the rows that caused the break-up.

Paul, George and Ringo – worth £550 million, £90 million and £70 million – could have added greatly to their fortunes.

Four years ago they turned down £113 million for 17 shows in America, Germany and Japan.

Beatles tell of yesterdays

Sir Paul McCartney: Announced the new book

The three surviving Beatles have reunited to write the story of their extraordinary years with the band.

Sir Paul McCartney, George Harrison and Ringo Starr are collaborating on the book, which will take the form of a joint autobiography giving a faithful account of the legendary band.

'It will dispel some of the myths and put the record straight, as every Tom, Dick and uncle of a friend has been writing books on the Beatles since 1963,' Sir Paul told the Sunday Telegraph.

Hundreds of statements made by John Lennon will be woven in to the three men's accounts, to complete the picture. His widow, Yoko Ono, will also get a quarter share of the expected £1bn profits, the paper says.

The book, 360 pages long, has taken six years to write and is predicted to go on sale in the autumn.

The three surviving Beatles, now in their late 50s, are said to have provided 1,200 photographs, many of them previously unpublished.

Sir Paul McCartney's spokesman, Geoff Baker, said: 'There have been around 300 – 400 books about the Beatles written, and in all but a few exceptions, the authors have never even met any of them.' He said the book, the Beatles Anthology, was 'the last word' on the Beatles.

'We're talking a huge volume of work, it's encyclopaedic – it weighs something like two kilos,' he said.

John Lennon: His writings have been 'woven in'

BBC NEWS

The way they were: Beatles in the early days

Mr Baker added: 'They hope it will put the record straight on a few things, for example the break-up of the band, that Paul was actually the last to leave.'

The autobiography will also disclose new information about the group's drug taking, their sexual exploits and rivalries. And Yoko Ono's influence will come under the spotlight. Many fans blamed her for luring Lennon away from the band.

Yoko Ono: Will receive a 'quarter share of profits'

The book will speak about more recent pressures, according to the Telegraph, disclosing that, four years ago, the three Beatles turned down an offer of £113 million to perform 17 concerts.

The Beatles Anthology is said to be due for publication in the UK and USA, with translations into dozens of languages, including Chinese.

Worldwide sales projections are put at more than 20 million.

Text level focus

1 A report's headline will usually show the angle of the report. Look back at the headlines of both reports.

  a What does each headline suggest its report will be about?

  b Just from the headlines, which report is biased, and against which person?

2 Biased texts usually try to affect their readers' views from the start, so the order in which they present information can be important.

  a How much of each report is about Yoko Ono and the money she will make? Where does each report place this information?

  b How does this affect the emphasis of each report?

3 The first half of the Mirror report ends with this quotation: 'But Paul and the boys are used to the system and they're long past begrudging Yoko the cash.'

  How would the article's emphasis change if this sentence was moved to the beginning of the article?

Sentence level focus

1 Newspaper reports start with a topic sentence, which outlines the basic story of the article. The topic sentence will usually answer some or all of the 'five Ws': who, what, where, when, why.

  a What answers does each topic sentence give to the 'five Ws'? Which ones does it not answer, and why?

  b How does this set the tone for each article?

2 Newspaper writers will select quotations to suit the angle of their report. Look at the quotations from the Beatles' spokesman in the two reports.

  a What do these quotations focus on in each article?

  b How do they reinforce the angle of each report?

Word level focus

1 Look at these extracts from the articles. Without looking at the texts again, decide which article each example comes from.

  a Yoko Ono will pocket more than £200 million

  b Yoko Ono: Will receive a quarter share of profits

  c The atonishing windfall for John Lennon's widow

  d The Beatles anthology has been in the pipeline for SIX YEARS

  e The book has taken six years to write

  f Yoko, Paul, George and Ringo will coin it

How could you tell which was from which article?

2 Emotive or opinion-based language can be used to bias a report's readers. Which of the highlighted phrases above reinforce the bias of the Mirror article? Try to explain how you think they do this.

Writing biased and objective texts

Story outline: a local company, AJAX Chemicals, has dumped 1000 gallons of waste into a nearby river – but it is not dangerous.

Write the headline and opening paragraph for a biased report and an objective (unbiased) one.

Objective report	Biased report
Researching and planning • Decide on what the basic story is – this needs to be obvious in the headline and opening paragraph.	**Researching and planning** • Decide on an angle to take in the headline and opening paragraph (such as suggesting AJAX Chemicals are irresponsible).
Advice on structure and language • Think about a headline that tells the idea of the story. • Begin with a topic sentence. • Avoid emotionally-charged language – keep it factual. • Repeat the story in the opening paragraph in a formal style.	**Advice on structure and language** • Think of a biased headline – probably sensational. • Begin with a topic sentence. • Use sensational and dramatic vocabulary. • Select facts and quotations to reinforce the angle of your report.
Drafting • Check that your report is neutral and balanced.	**Drafting** • Make sure that your report is one-sided and tries to sway the reader's opinion.
Revising • Ensure that your style is formal. • Do your headline and opening sound completely factual?	**Revising** • Do your headline and opening put across a clear angle?

Both sides of the story

This unit looks at discursive writing and in particular at essays. These text types are all about presenting a balanced discussion by showing both points of view.

 **Exploring discursive writing**

Look at these two texts:

A

Some people believe that homeless people cause themselves to be homeless. They think that someone living on the streets has chosen this instead of trying to get a job to pay rent and bills or has not worked hard enough at making family relationships work. On the other hand, there are those who think that people have no option but to become homeless because of unemployment, high rents and bills. Added to this are complicated home backgrounds and a lack of suitable hostels to cater for those without anywhere to live.

B

We believe that hunting wild animals with dogs is cruel. Where there is proven need to control the numbers of animals such as deer, foxes and mink, we believe that there are alternative methods which are much more humane and effective than hunting with dogs.

Now get into small groups and discuss these points for each text:

- Does it have a neutral point of view (showing both sides) or a biased one (one-sided)?

- Does the writer use discourse markers (words or phrases which sequence a text or show a shift in emphasis, e.g. 'firstly', 'however') to show stages of the discussion?

- Is the writer involved in the text? (Look for 'I', 'we', etc.)

- What tense is mainly used?

In your study you might have noticed that:

- Text A shows both sides of the argument but text B is biased – it only presents one side (that hunting with dogs is wrong). So text A is a discursive text, and text B is not.

- Text A uses discourse markers like 'Some people believe that' and 'On the other hand' to make the stages of the argument clear.

- Text A's writer is neutral, not taking a side but text B uses 'we' to show that this is a specific group's opinion.

- Both texts are written in the present tense as they are examining issues that are relevant now.

 The key to writing discursive texts

When you are writing a discursive text, you should:

- show both sides of the argument

- use discourse markers to show which side's view you are presenting when

- write in the present tense – as essays usually deal with events that are of current interest

- avoid using 'I' or 'we' to make it clear that it is balanced, rather than opinion-based.

You may also show your own view as part of the summing-up of the arguments.

Essay on GM foods

This essay looks at the debate on genetically modified foods and whether they are a good or bad thing. Essays like this appear in newspapers, magazines and journals.

GM foods – good or bad?

The last few years have seen a great deal of argument and discussion over genetically modified (GM) foods. The battle lines have been drawn over whether they are a good or a bad thing. Certainly the decision whether to go ahead with genetically modified foods could affect food supplies and the environment – and clearly it would have an impact on the world of farming.

GM foods are created from crops that have had their basic genes changed. A plant's genes decide things such as the plant's size and flavour, and resistance to disease. In genetic modification, a scientist picks out genes for specific characteristics in one plant, and transplants those genes into a different plant species. The new plant will then grow with the characteristics that have been 'borrowed' from the other plant because of its new genes. This may make it bigger, change its flavour, or make it able to cope with less water, for example.

However, this idea has sparked much debate and disagreement throughout the United Kingdom.

Pro-GM technologists claim that this new technology is nothing to worry about. It is no more than an extension of the kinds of breeding and crossbreeding that farmers have been using for generations. However, anti-GM campaigners say that it is a very different idea from this practice, and it has not been properly explored, so its risks and wider implications are not yet known.

Some GM technology is about producing pesticide-resistant crops, so that fewer chemicals have to be sprayed on them. Some people believe that this will benefit the environment and make the food much better to eat. Contrary to this, others say that the effects on the environment are likely to be negative, as bees, birds and the wind might carry GM pollen to weeds which would then become pesticide-resistant 'superweeds', so more chemicals would be needed to control them. Non-GM crops might also be affected, so consumers would no longer know which foods were GM and which were not. Furthermore, the wildlife that co-exists with crops might be badly affected by eating the modified plants.

Many organizations are in support of GM crops, arguing that they can produce more, much better and cheaper food which could solve the problems of feeding developing countries. A recent report from the Nuffield Council on Bioethics points out that GM technology, if used properly, could play an important part in producing more food for areas that need it badly. Many developing countries produce too few crops, often because of problems of climate, disease and pest control. It is estimated that 100 million people are starving in the world – by enabling the poorer nations to grow more, better crops, GM technology could help. On the other hand, economists argue that we already produce enough food to feed the whole world: the problem is distribution, not production. GM technology is owned by a small number of companies, and campaigners fear that if GM crops are grown widely, these companies could end up owning and controlling the majority of the world's food supply.

People and companies in favour of GM technology claim that anti-GM campaigners are misguided; they do not or will not consider the advantages and instead use scare-mongering and propaganda against good science. Moreover, they are costing the government and farmers hundreds of thousands of pounds in ruined crops that have been sabotaged. Anti-GM campaigners point out studies which suggest that eating GM foods might have devastating side effects on the health of people and on the environment, and say that it is wiser to be safe now than be sorry later.

To sum up, the pro-GM side argue that this technology will help us feed the world's increasing population and improve the environment. The anti-GM side say that the technology has not been well-enough tested to be sure that it is safe for people, and fear that its impact on the environment could be disastrous, with the added possibility of the GM companies controlling the whole world's food supply. Many countries throughout the world have successfully introduced GM, while in the UK a number of field trials are being carried out (year 2000) but no commercial crops are being grown. Only time will really tell us which approach is best and which side of the debate is right. Until we know for sure, the arguments will continue.

Text level focus

1 The title of an essay should introduce the subject. How does this essay's title do this?

2 Discursive texts usually begin with a statement of the issue and a preview of the main arguments. Does this text work in this way?

3 Discursive texts are structured along the lines of:

- all the arguments for + supporting evidence
- all the arguments against + supporting evidence

or alternatively

- argument/counter argument (both with evidence), one point at a time

How does the writer of this text structure the arguments?

4 Key features of a good essay are:

- using statistics
- quoting from reports
- using personal testimonies (saying what qualified people think).

Which of these features can you spot in the essay?

5 The essay is written in the third person ('it', 'they', 'people', etc.). What would happen if the writer used the first person 'I'?

6 A good discursive essay will make it clear what is fact and what is opinion. Look at these examples and for each one decide whether they are fact, opinion, or a mixture of both:

a Pro-GM technologists claim that this new technology is nothing to worry about

b GM technology is owned by a small number of companies

c Other people say that the effects on the environment are likely to be negative, as bees, birds and the wind might carry GM pollen to weeds

d They are costing the government and farmers hundreds of pounds in ruined crops that have been sabotaged

e In the UK a number of field trials are being carried out (year 2000)

Sentence level focus

1 The writer rarely uses simple sentences in the text. Why do you think they do this?

2 Discursive texts use discourse markers to lead the reader through the stages of the discussion. In this essay, they are used in three different ways:

a Discourse markers that show an opposite point of view, e.g. 'however'.
Find two more examples.

b Discourse markers that give points on the same view, e.g. 'also'.
Find two more examples.

c A discourse marker to draw the writing to a close and finish off the discussion.
Find this example.

d How important are discourse markers in the discussion as a whole? (Think about how they help the reader.)

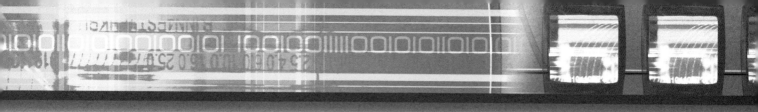

3 The writer of this essay uses a mixture of active and passive sentence structures. For example:

Active sentence – A scientist picks out genes for specific characteristics in one plant, and transplants those genes into a different plant species.

Here, we can see that the scientist is the person performing the action.

Passive sentence – GM foods are created from crops that have had their basic genes changed.

This does not say who has performed the action. (Sometimes this is done because it's not really important exactly who did it.)

a Look at these examples from the essay and decide whether they are active or passive and then explain how you can tell. You could copy your answers out into a copy of the chart below.

Active	Passive	How can you tell?
	The battle lines have been drawn over whether they are a good or bad thing.	Does not say who has drawn the battle lines.

- Pro-GM technologists claim that this new technology is nothing to worry about.
- However, anti-GM campaigners say that it is a very different idea from this …
- … it has not been properly explored
- It is estimated that …
- … 100 million people are starving in the world.
- Economists argue that we already produce enough food to feed the whole world.

b Now take one active phrase or sentence and make it passive and one passive sentence and make it active. For example:

Passive – The battle lines have been drawn over whether they are a good or bad thing.

Active – Pro-GM and anti-GM technologists have drawn battle lines over whether it is a good or bad thing

Word level focus

1 This is a scientific discussion and many words would be too complex for a younger reader. Try to explain what these words mean for a younger reader:

technologists   devastating

traditional   propaganda

sabotaged

Writing a discursive essay

Capital punishment is illegal in the United Kingdom but widely practised in other countries of the world. It is a subject that sparks great controversy amongst people and really whether or not it is acceptable is down to the individual.

Your teacher will give you some material to help you work on this discursive essay:

Capital punishment: for or against?

You need to present a balanced view of the subject here – as a good discursive essay does (look back at the one that you have studied).

Research and planning

- Using the material and your own ideas, decide on how to structure your points (either the arguments for first, and then those against, or for and against following each other).

- Try to select which areas you are going to focus on – it's a huge topic, so you will have to leave bits out.

Advice on structure and planning

- Open with a statement of the issue and a preview of the main arguments.

- Go through your points, remembering to use evidence to support each view (statistics, quoting qualified people, quoting reports).

- Finish with a summary and conclusion.

- Use the present tense.

- Avoid using 'I'.

- Use discourse markers to link ideas and show contrasts: words such as 'furthermore', 'however'.

- You can decide whether to give your own opinion – but if you do, only give it right at the end, as part of the summing-up.

Drafting

- Check that your points balance.

- Avoid making the essay too long as people will not want to read it.

Revising

- Check each other's work and see if your essay is objective (not taking a side but looking at the issue as a whole).

Explain yourself!

We give and use explanations every day. Think of all the times just today that you have explained something to someone or vice versa.

 Exploring explanations

Working with a partner, write a short explanation for him/her on one of the following topics.

1 Why do we need vitamins?

2 Why do we need sleep?

Write your explanation in full sentences, for example: 'We need vitamins…'

You probably carried on with 'because' or 'so that'. This is a typical feature in explanatory texts.

These texts work through telling the reader logical and causal connections between points (in other words why and how things happen). Typical causal connectives are:

- **We have seasons because the Earth's axis is tilted…**
- **But the amount of rain that falls varies, so some tropical places have just two seasons…**

Other typical causal connectives to look out for are 'therefore', and 'to/in order to'.

Now look at the two explanatory texts on the next page and as you study them, think about the following questions:

- What is the purpose of each text?
- Which tense is used and why?
- Do the texts follow a logical sequence?
- How do the writers connect ideas from point to point?
- What sort of words do the writers use to show why things happen?
- Do the writers' own opinions come across to you as a reader?

A

Some people wanted to stay Catholics. The most famous objectors were Thomas More, who had been Henry's Chancellor, and John Fisher, Bishop of Rochester. Both men were executed in 1535 because they refused to accept Henry as Head of the Church.

At first most people were not alarmed because church services did not change and churches looked as colourful as ever. The change seemed to be just a theory or idea. It did not affect people's lives in a practical way. Then, in 1536, Thomas Cromwell began to close monasteries all over England. This Dissolution of the Monasteries helped to cause a great rebellion, the Pilgrimage of Grace.

The pilgrims were northerners, rich and poor, men and women. Many had lost jobs in monasteries or on monastery farms. The poorest had depended on the monks for food and money. Now they wondered how they would survive. Others joined the rebellion because they did not want to leave the Roman Catholic Church.

B

A typical population curve – bacteria

It is easiest to study population growth by looking at simple organisms such as bacteria. They can be grown in a fermenter. Bacteria are put into a nutrient solution in the fermenter and kept warm. They reproduce and the number of cells can be measured.

The graph shows how the population changes.

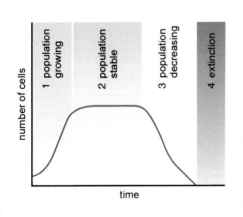

1 At first there is plenty of food and space and so the bacteria reproduce quickly. The population grows rapidly.

2 Gradually there is less food to go round and the bacteria do not reproduce so quickly. More of them die. The population becomes stable. The number of new bacteria is the same as the number of bacteria that die.

3 The population starts to decrease. This is because the food supply is being used up, and waste products from the bacteria are building up and poisoning them.

4 Eventually all the bacteria may die, and the population becomes extinct.

You should have spotted that:

- Each text's purpose is to explain (and also inform).

- Text A is written in the past tense (because it is about history), while text B is in the present tense (as it is about a process which commonly happens).

- Both extracts are impersonal – you get no idea of what the writer is like as the focus is on the topic and the explanation, not the writer's thoughts about it.

- Both texts use conjunctions like 'so' and 'because' which connect the discussion together.

- Text B uses temporal connectives such as 'at first', 'gradually', 'eventually' to lead the reader through the sequence.

The key to writing explanantions

So if you are writing an explanation, you should:

- write in the present tense (or the past if you are explaining something in history)

- use linking words to sequence the explanation

- use an impersonal style

- make logical connections between cause and effect.

You can also present explanations with diagrams and illustrations to reinforce the text.

Children's encyclopedia

As this text is written for a younger reader it has to be well presented, easy to follow and clear in its language use.

Midnight Sun

Close to the North and South Poles, there are places where the Sun never sets for days or weeks in midsummer. These places experience the Midnight Sun. In midwinter, the opposite happens and the Sun never rises. This effect happens because the Earth's axis is tilted. The places that get the Midnight Sun lie inside the Arctic and Antarctic circles. The Antarctic has no permanent inhabitants, but people living near and inside the Arctic Circle have to adapt to long periods of continuous daylight or night-time.

Seasons

As each season arrives, the length of daylight and the daily weather alter. Summer days are longer and warmer, while winter ones are shorter and cooler. Throughout the year, the different seasons bring changes to the world around us.

of its rays. In autumn, the days shorten again, many trees drop their leaves, and the weather gets cooler as winter approaches.

Near the Equator, the number of hours of daylight does not change much through the year and it stays hot all year round. But the amount of rain that falls varies, so some tropical places have just two seasons: a wet one and a dry one. The seasonal changes are more extreme the further you are from the Equator. Near the Poles, there

▲ This time-lapse photograph of the Midnight Sun was taken over northern Norway in midsummer. It shows the position of the Sun in the sky at one-hour intervals. Although the Sun is low in the sky at midnight, it never drops below the horizon.

In spring, after the short days of winter, the amount of daily sunshine increases as the Sun climbs higher in the sky. Summer is the warmest time of the year. The higher the Sun is, the stronger the warming effect

are enormous differences between the length of winter and summer days, but it never gets really warm because the Sun is not very high in the sky, even in midsummer.

The changing seasons

The Earth takes one year to travel around the Sun. We have seasons because the Earth's axis (an imaginary line going through the North and South Poles) is tilted to its path round the Sun at a angle of 23½°. From about 21 March to 21 September, the North Pole is tilted towards the Sun and places in the northern hemisphere have spring followed by summer. At the same time the South Pole faces away from the Sun. From September to March, the North Pole is tilted away from the Sun. Places in the northern hemisphere have autumn and winter while the southern hemisphere has spring and summer.

Each year, on or near 21 March and 23 September, the hours of daylight and darkness everywhere in the world are equal. These days are known as the spring and autumn equinoxes (equinox means 'equal night'). At midday on the equinoxes, the Sun is directly overhead at places on the Equator. The days when the number of hours of daylight is greatest and smallest also have a special name. They are called the solstices and fall on or about 21 June and 21 December.

find out more
Arctic
Climate
Earth

▼ Places on Earth receive different amounts of sunlight during the year as the Earth travels around the Sun.

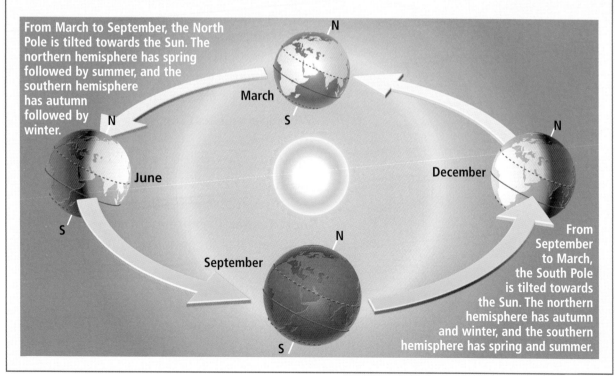

From March to September, the North Pole is tilted towards the Sun. The northern hemisphere has spring followed by summer, and the southern hemisphere has autumn followed by winter.

N

March

S

N

June

S

September

N

S

N

December

From September to March, the South Pole is tilted towards the Sun. The northern hemisphere has autumn and winter, and the southern hemisphere has spring and summer.

Text level focus

1 Explanations need to be carefully presented for easy use. Look at these presentational devices (which are meant to make the text easier to use and to look attractive on the page) – where would you say each one appears on the page?

- topic paragraph
- margin notes
- main text
- find out more panel
- captions
- diagrams
- illustrations
- headings
- subheadings

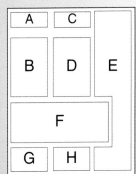
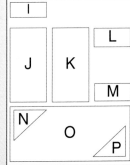

2 The sequence of an explanation needs to be easy to follow. Here, the writer helps the reader by using temporal connectives – words or phrases which give an indication of time, such as 'throughout the year', 'in spring'.

a Find three more examples of temporal connectives.

b Now look what happens when you remove these from a paragraph. Take paragraph 2 and rewrite it without the temporal connectives. How clear is the text now?

3 Explanatory texts are usually written in an impersonal style – the focus is on the writer explaining something, rather than giving their opinion. Look at this extract from the text which has been made more personal:

Near the Poles, I have been told that there are enormous differences between the length of winter and summer days, but it never gets really warm because the Sun is not very high in the sky, even in midsummer. I think this must be a bit depressing if it is always cold there.

Why does this text not work in a personal style?

4 On a scale of 1 to 5 (1 the lowest and 5 the highest) how clear would you say this explanation text is as a whole? Explain in a short answer. If you don't think it's very clear, can you suggest how to improve it?

Sentence level focus

1 In the introductory activities you noticed that the history textbook extract was written in the past tense. Most explanation texts are written in the present tense.

Why would this text on the seasons not work in the past tense? Try reworking the opening paragraph in the past tense to see what happens. What do you notice?

Word level focus

1 The writer uses quite a lot of comparatives and superlatives in this explanation.

a Look at these examples from the text and decide whether they are comparatives or superlatives:

- Summer days are longer and warmer, while winter ones are shorter and cooler.
- The higher the sun is, the stronger the warming effect of its rays.
- The days when the number of hours of daylight is greatest and smallest also have a special name.

b Why does the writer use these? Select the best answer:

- The writer wants to show off what he/she can do.
- The writer is trying to compare seasons to make the information clear for the reader.
- The writer thinks that the reader does not know that it is different in each season.

> Comparatives are used to compare two people or things – they end in -er, e.g. 'bigger'.
>
> Superlatives are used to compare more than two things or people – they end in -est, e.g. 'biggest'.

Writing an explanation

You are now going to produce your own explanation text for a CD-Rom (aimed at the general public) using the key features that you have learned about in this unit. Take one of the topics below to work on:

- how something works (such as a telephone, a satellite, or a television – you might need to research this beforehand)

- a scientific procedure (you might have done something in Science that you could use here)

- an explanation of how something happens (such as coastal erosion, global warming, or perhaps a topic that you have studied in Geography).

Whatever you choose, make sure you use the key features in your writing. The topic is important but not as much as your writing.

Research and planning

- Get your material together – remember that this will be for the general reader, so do not overload them with information.

Advice on structure and language

- Think about presentational devices to make the page look clear and attractive.

- Use logical steps and lead the reader through the sequence with temporal connectives.

- Use causal connectives to show how and why things happen.

- Write in the present tense (all the options above will use this tense).

- Use an impersonal style – including your opinions will make the explanation less clear and convincing.

Drafting

- Start by thinking about how to organize the material – short paragraphs might be better than long ones.

- Decide how to help the reader find the way around the text.

- Start with a general statement of the subject e.g. 'Over the last few decades, the earth's temperature has warmed up…'

- Check that you are giving an overview of the subject.

Revising

- Ask someone to read your text to see if it flows. Is it detailed enough? Does it need to be made less technical?

Say it write!

Exploring spoken and written language

Have you ever thought about how differently you express yourself when you are talking and when you write?

When you write, you think quite hard about what to say and how to express it. But in most situations, we pay a lot less attention to exactly how we express ourselves in speech. We 'think on our feet' – and this gives spoken language some characteristics which written language doesn't have. For example, in speech we include words that would not appear in writing. We tend to use specific:

- greetings
- fillers
- hesitations.

Look at this list and for each one decide which category above it belongs to.

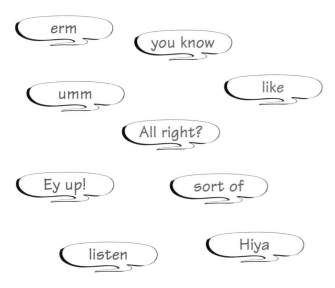

erm

you know

umm

like

All right?

Ey up!

sort of

listen

Hiya

Can you think of any more?

Now look in more detail at the differences between written and spoken texts.

A Extract from a chat show

Interviewer	So when did you realize that you wanted to be an actor?
Guest	Well, erm, I guess I must have been in, erm, my mid teens, yeah cos' I remember telling my mom that I was going to be in, like, a hit movie some day.
Interviewer	So it came true.
Guest	Sure. I sometimes find it weird that this all kind of happened, you know. I mean, one day you're just a kid in school, just a kid, you know, bikes and... and the next, well, you're all over magazines and on TV constantly. Definitely a weird kind of experience.

B Written version of the interview

Interviewer	So when did you realize that you wanted to be an actor?
Guest	I must have been in my mid teens, as I remember telling my mother that I was going to be in a film one day.
Interviewer	So it came true.
Guest	Yes. I sometimes find it strange that this all happened. One day I was just a pupil in school and the next I was in all sorts of magazines and on television constantly. It was definitely an odd kind of experience.

Answer these questions to compare the texts. What do you notice about:

- fillers and hesitations?
- use of vocabulary (which is informal and which is more formal)?
- the structure of sentences?
- the length of the two versions (which one is shorter and more to the point)?

You probably noticed that:

- Version A has a lot of fillers and hesitations, which have been removed in version B to make the text shorter and clearer.
- In version A the writer uses more informal vocabulary such as 'weird' and 'mom'. In version B the language has been made more formal: 'odd' and 'mother'.
- Version A's sentences are very disjointed, reflecting the way we speak and change direction as we go along. Version B is more structured.
- Version B is shorter and more to the point as it removes hesitations, fillers and sidetracks.

 # The key to writing down spoken language

If you are changing spoken language into a written form, you need to:

- control informal vocabulary or replace it with more formal words and phrases
- tighten up sentence structures
- remove repetition of words or phrases
- remove hesitations
- remove fillers.

Docusoap

Guns and Roses is a docusoap: a TV programme which combines two genres:

- A documentary that explains and follows a situation or process with a narrator

- A soap opera that follows a series of characters.

Guns and Roses follows a group of female army cadets including Kat Astley, Andrea Madgwick, and Lisa Potts through a one-year training course at Sandhurst to become officers in the Royal Artillery.

Guns and Roses

Voice over	In just over 10 weeks all-female 11 platoon will finish their year-long army officer training course.
	Although they are going to be officers, they still have to master basic military skills like battlefield first aid, and that's something that Cambridge graduate Kat Astley finds a real challenge.
Kat	Erm, I hope if someone found me with horrendous injuries that they'd be able to deal with it better than I can but erm, depends what it is.
VO	But there's another test that everyone is dreading, especially Andrea Madgwick.
Andrea	Getting my respirator on in nine seconds 'cos I've been practising all morning and frankly it's impossible so I feel I may be doing it again. I've done it once today and err, these gloves are about, sort of 50 million sizes too big and I know in bad weather it'll be beneficial but it doesn't help and err you're sort of fiddling with everything and everything falls off and yes. I think in a real life situation that would be my downfall.
Officer	Gas, gas, gas!

VO	The reason they have nine seconds is that in a nerve gas attack they'd be dead in ten.
Officer	(counting) 7, 8, 9.
VO	Here Andrea can have a second chance.
Officer	Stand by – Gas, gas, gas!
	7, 8, 9.
	Well done, good. Get yourselves sorted out.
Andrea	Those gloves, yeah, it's a nightmare and so I fumble 'cos I panic and it's definitely more haste less speed definitely but hopefully we're all right ha ha
VO	Lisa Potts needs a second attempt too.
Officer	Gas, gas, gas!
	7, 8, 9 – Forget it ladies.
Lisa	That's it, failed completely. Oh it's such a stupid flipping thing to do, you know what I mean? It's so simple but I couldn't... by the time I'd done that I was on 7 seconds and there's no way and then the rifle's in the way and everything, not that it should be a problem because we should be able to do it and everything. I'm really not happy now.
VO	Everyone who fails today will resit in three weeks. Failure then could mean retaking the whole term.
	A good officer can lead even when they are frightened, so the cadets have to learn to confront their fears.
Officer	Some of you will be scared of heights, some of you won't be, some of you may be following this, ha, ha

VO	Andrea is terrified of heights.
Andrea	D'you realize I have nightmares in the holidays and err about it and over leave but err I've kind of resigned myself to the fact that I have to go up there. I'm not sure, to be fair, if I'm going to get over but I'll give it my best shot.
VO	She has to cross the high wire nine metres above the ground and there's no safety net. Someone who understands her fear despite having made almost 100 parachute jumps is Sergeant Steve Wallis.
Steve	I do know what it's like to freeze and then have to think to yourself you've got no other way down, I'm either… for me personally it was to let myself down in front of the rest of the platoon so that'll make you go forward anyway.
Andrea	(up ladder about to get on high wire and crying) I can't slide across that, I'm not doing it, I'm not…
VO of Steve	but if the fear is deeply set in, maybe there's a chance that there's nothing gonna stop you
Andrea	There's no way I'm gonna get across there. I will not be OK I'm sorry…
Officer	(up ladder with her) Just stand up there. Miss Madgwick, stop talking like this, get in there, confront it and do it. Left arm on cable, that's it, well done.
Andrea	(later in room) You persuade yourself it's fine, you get to the high wire and you think yeah, I can't actually physically do this and it err panics you and you can't reason with yourself err and it's pathetic, I mean it is, it's pathetic ha, ha
	And when I got up on the high wire it was OK so I was quite pleased with that but err, it's a very frustrating fear to have and although I did get across it you still think, well, you know err, I didn't fly across it ha, ha
VO	But she's impressed company commander Major Harry Empe with her courage.

Text level focus

1 Explain how you can tell that this is a docusoap.

2 A documentary's purpose is to inform and explain. A soap opera's purpose is to entertain. Do you think this docusoap fulfills both purposes?

3 The sentence rhythms of the narrator are controlled and brief whereas those of the people in the film are longer, more disjointed and mixed. Why is there a contrast between the narrator and the other people?

Sentence level focus

1 Look at this extract from Andrea's speech:

Getting my respirator on in nine seconds 'cos I've been practising all morning and frankly it's impossible so I feel I may be doing it again. I've done it once today and err, these gloves are about, sort of 50 million sizes too big and I know in bad weather it'll be beneficial but it doesn't help and err you're sort of fiddling with everything and everything falls off and yes. I think in a real life situation that would be my downfall.

Andrea is clearly thinking about a number of different things as she speaks. It looks confusing when it is written down – because in writing we expect thoughts to be organized. But in speech, we say things as they occur to us, jumping from one subject to another, and often without forming proper sentences.

a Rework this speech so that it is more logical in writing – use full stops, new paragraphs, etc. You may need to edit some parts out (they might not be too relevant).

b How have your changes altered the tone of what Andrea says?

Word level focus

1 Because the recruits' speech is spontaneous, there are many distinctive elements of spoken language here. Pick out words or examples that you would not expect to find in written English.

Writing spoken and written texts

Interview a friend or member of your family and try to record what they say on tape. It only needs to be about two minutes long – so don't make it a long interview.

Researching and planning

- Try to choose an interviewee and a subject that you will find interesting – you will end up listening to the interview quite a few times.

- Plan at least three questions, as you don't know how long they will take to answer each one.

- Do the recording in a quiet room, and make sure there is no music playing in the background: you will need to hear what they say very clearly.

Drafting

- Make a transcript: play the whole thing through once or twice, then start listening to it in short sections, writing each part down as you go.

- When you have written down a part, listen to that section again to make sure you got it right. Remember to write down everything they say, including the hesitations – and don't correct their grammar!

- Using the transcript, go through it and highlight all the areas of non-standard English that would need changing in a written text – look for hesitations, greetings, fillers, etc.

Revising

- Now rewrite the interview in formal standard English.

- Finally write a short summary of the changes that you had to make and what differences you notice between spoken and written language.

Acknowledgements

We are grateful to the following for permission to reprint copyright material:

British Broadcasting Corporation for transcribed extract from World Service Radio News broadcast, Sunday, 2 July 2000 and for BBC On-line News article, 'Beatles Tell of Yesterday', July 2000; **Black and White Publishing Ltd** for extract from Billy Adams: *Ewan McGregor – The Unauthorized Biography* (1998); **Blackwell Publishers** for Charlotte Bronte's letter from T J Wise and J A Symington (eds): *The Brontes: Their Lives, Friendships and Correspondence* (The Shakespeare Head Bronte, vols i-iii, Blackwell, 1932-8); **Bloomsbury Publishing Plc** for extract from Melissa Muller: *Anne Frank, the Biography* (Metropolitan, 1998, Bloomsbury, 1999), first published in German as *Das Madchen Anne Frank* (Paul List Verlag), copyright © 1998 by Melissa Muller, translated by Rita and Robert Kimber, translation copyright © 1998 by Metropolitan Books; **The Cybernaut Project** for review of 'Tarzan' by Lisa Freinkman, published on the web site, primarycontact.net; **Andre Deutsch Ltd** for extract from David Beckham: *My Story* (Manchester United Books, an imprint of Andre Deutsch, 1998); **Bill Duffin and the Imperial War Museum** (Department of Documents) for letter from Murray Duffin to his family, Royal Navy, HMS Arrow, 6 May 1982, from Imperial War Museum collection; **Nicky Hayes** for extract from advice to students on tackling stress published on http://www.nickyhayes.co.uk/nicky/exams; **Her Majesty's Stationery Office** for extracts from leaflet 'Are Your Children Safe in the Kitchen' (URN 98/555, Department of Trade and Industry). Crown copyright is reproduced with the permission of the Controller of Her Majesty's Stationery Office; **The Home Office** for fire safety leaflet: 'Get a Plan' (FL5, Home Office, March 2000); **The Baroness Mallalieu** for extract from speech made in October 1997 at Countryside Rally in London's Hyde Park; **Mirror Syndication International** for Voice of the Mirror editorial: 'Mere Words Won't Stop the Violence', *The Mirror*, 20.6.00, and article by Kevin O'Sullivan: 'Yoko to Make £200m from Beatles Book', *The Mirror*, 3.4.00; **News International Syndication** for front page headline from article by Chris Pharo and Ian Hepburn, *The Sun*, 21.7.00; Oxford University Press for article on 'Seasons' from *Oxford Children's Encyclopedia of Our World* (OUP, 1999); extract from 'The Effects of Religious Change: Henry VIII', in *The Making of the United Kingdom* by Charles Maltman and Ian Dawson (OUP, 1992); and extract and graph from 'Population Growth' in *World of Science Book 3* by Graham Booth, Bob McDuell and John Sears (OUP, 1999); **The Random House Group Ltd** for extract from Brian Keenan: *An Evil Cradling* (Hutchinson, 1992); **RSPCA** for extracts from information leaflet: 'All Alone?'; **Margaret Thatcher** for extract from speech, 'The Falklands Factor', addressed to a rally of Conservative Women, Cheltenham, 3 July 1982; **WWF-UK** for extract from Black Rhino campaign letter, text by Carlson Marketing Group.

The short extracts used on the following pages are also taken from copyright works:

p 5 from *The Snowman* by Raymond Briggs (Hamish Hamilton, 1978); p 6 from film review of 'Gladiator' by Barry Norman in *The Radio Times*, 20-26.5.00; p 6 from *2wentys* holiday brochure 2000, First Choice Holidays & Flights Ltd; p 7 'Volcanoes' from *The Earth and Beyond* by Chris Oxlad (Science Topics, Heinemann, 1998); p 14 from 'The Score: Facts About Drugs', Health Education Authority, 1998; p 41 from leaflet on asthma, National Union of Teachers; p 42 from *Eyewitness Guide: Sharks* (Dorling Kindersley, 1992); p 79 from film review of 'Romeo Must Die' in *The Daily Telegraph*, 13.10.00; p 79 from film review of 'Billy Elliot' in *Heat*, 3.11.00; p 103 from 'Back the Ban' letter, RSPCA, 1999.

We have tried to trace and contact all copyright holders before publication. If notified the publishers will be pleased to rectify any errors or omissions at the earliest opportunity.

Photograph Credits

Cover photographs – Digital Vision and Image Bank

p.7 Corel; p.21 Image Bank; p.22 Image Bank; p.29 PA Photos; p.37 Which Consumers Association; p.41 Corbis; p.42 Corbis; p.43 Colin Varndell (left), Ardea/Eric Dracesco (right), NHPA/Andy Rouse (bottom right); p.46 Network/Jillian Edelstein (right), Rex Features/Kosta Alexander (left); p.47 Rex Features (middle), Popperfoto/Ian Waldie (right); p.49 Corbis; p.53 QA Photos Limited (top), Rex Features/Sipa/Niviere (bottom); p.55 BBC Picture Library; p.57 S & R Greenhill; p.60 Still Pictures; p.61 Bridgeman Art Library; p. 64 EPA/Popperfoto/Adam Butler; p.65 Popperfoto/Reuter/D Joiner; p.74 WWF UK/David Lawson (middle), WWF UK/Iain Derrick (bottom); p.75 WWF UK/KWS (top), WWF UK/David Lawson (bottom); p.81 Ronald Grant Archive/Walt Disney; p.83 Ronald Grant Archive/Walt Disney; p.85 Corel; p.88 Popperfoto/Reuter/Peter Kujundzic; p.89 Rex Features; p.91 Network/Peter Jordan; p.96 Corbis; p.98 Corbis (middle), Rex Features/Harry Goodwin (right); p.99 Rex Features/David Hogan (top), Rex Features/David Magnus (bottom); p.100 Rex Features/Harry Goodwin (top), Rex Features/Tim Rooke (bottom); p.103 Corbis; p.105 Rex Features; p.106 Popperfoto/Reuter; p.114 Gettyone Stone; p.122 BBC Photograph Library.

Illustrations are by :
p.12 Gillian Martin; p.13 Stefan Chabluk; p 33 Darrell Warner; p.67 Tim Clarey